# BIG IDEAS
# FOR
# CURIOUS MINDS

First published in 2018 by The School of Life
First published in the USA in 2019
70 Marchmont Street, London WC1N 1AB

Copyright © The School of Life 2018
Illustrations © Anna Doherty
Designed and typeset by Studio Katie Kerr

Printed in Italy by L.E.G.O. S.p.A

The School of Life is a resource for helping us understand
ourselves, for improving our relationships, our careers and
our social lives — as well as helping us find calm and get
more out of our leisure hours. We do this through creating
films, workshops, books and gifts.

www.theschooloflife.com

ISBN 978-1-9997471-4-5

10 9 8 7 6 5

AN INTRODUCTION TO PHILOSOPHY

# BIG IDEAS FOR CURIOUS MINDS

THE SCHOOL OF LIFE PRESS

# INSIDE THIS BOOK

# WHAT IS PHILOSOPHY?

Philosophy is quite a mysterious subject that most people don't know anything about. The average school doesn't teach it, the average adult does not understand it, and the whole subject can seem odd and kind of unnecessary. That's a real pity because, in fact, philosophy has a lot to teach everyone, whatever their age. It might even be the most important subject you will ever study. This book wants to open the door for you—to show you what philosophy is all about, and how it can help you to understand life.

The word 'philosophy' itself gives us a bit of a clue as to why the subject matters. It's originally a word from Ancient Greek: the first part, *philo*, means 'love' (*philately* means the love of stamps). The second part, which comes from the word *sophia*, means 'wisdom'. So, when you put the two parts together—*philo-sophy*—it literally means 'the love of wisdom'.

Philosophy helps us to live wise lives. But what does 'wisdom' mean? It's not very obvious, at first. Is being wise just about being clever? No, it's much more than that. It's about being sensible, kind, calm and accepting of how life can sometimes be (which isn't always perfect, and sometimes really quite hard).

To get a better idea of what wisdom might involve, we can think about its opposite: not being wise. Imagine that your mum loses her keys. There are unwise ways she might deal with this. Maybe she starts shouting at other people: 'Who moved my car keys?' (even though probably no one did move them). Or maybe she gets into a panic and throws herself onto the sofa, moaning that she's a complete idiot and that her entire life is ruined. Poor mum!

What would a wiser mum do? Instead of ranting and raving, or starting to panic straight away, she would think: 'Well, car keys do tend to get lost from time to time. I must have put them somewhere... maybe they're in the coat I was wearing yesterday.' She could ask (calmly) if you had seen them, and she might even laugh about how silly she was to forget where she'd put them.

There are lots of situations where you can see the difference between unwise and wise ways of dealing with stuff that happens. There are lots of problems, both big and small, in everyone's life—including yours, too, of course. We can never get rid of them entirely (though we try hard), but we can all get better at how we deal with our problems.

We can try not to get angry so often, try to shout less, and try not to panic or hurt the people we love. Philosophy tries to help us act more wisely when facing the problems in our lives that we can't do much about.

# WISE AND UNWISE RESPONSES

**YOU LOSE A GAME OF CONNECT FOUR TO YOUR BROTHER**

UNWISE RESPONSES

Accuse your brother of cheating
(though you know they didn't really)

Tell everyone how much you hate the
game you were playing

Feel that it's incredibly important that you
lost, and that you won't get over it for ages

*or*

WISE RESPONSES

Remember it's only a game, and that whether
you have good luck says nothing about what
you're like as a person

Remind yourself that you're bound to win
some other time and that there are other,
more important, things in your life

**A FRIEND ISN'T VERY NICE TO YOU**

UNWISE RESPONSES

Be horrible back to them

Feel that maybe you deserve
to be treated badly

*or*

WISE RESPONSES

Wonder what might be
upsetting them

Tell them calmly that they hurt your
feelings, and ask what's wrong

# A CAR JOURNEY IS VERY LONG

UNWISE RESPONSES

Keep on asking when you'll get there

Tell everyone that you are
very, very bored

Complain that the journey is too
long every couple of minutes

*or*

WISE RESPONSES

Admit to yourself that it's going to
take ages no matter what you do

Look at things out of the window
and make up a game or story

Design the perfect house or submarine
in your head to pass the time

---

# YOU DON'T LIKE WHAT YOU'VE BEEN GIVEN FOR DINNER

UNWISE RESPONSES

Shout about how disgusting it is

Throw it on the floor

Refuse to eat it

*or*

WISE RESPONSES

Politely explain what you would
prefer to have instead

Offer to help prepare something
else another time

Keep in mind that whoever made
dinner didn't mean to disappoint
you, and that it might hurt their
feelings if you complain

## YOU ACCIDENTALLY SPOIL A DRAWING YOU WERE DOING

Tear it up and stamp on it

Promise never to do another drawing again

*or*

Try again—and eventually you will do it better

Make a feature of the mistake. You could turn a smudge into a shadow or an ink blot into a spider — sometimes, what we think of as an 'error' can be the start of something even more interesting

---

## YOU HAVE TO GO TO BED AND YOU'RE NOT TIRED

Scream about how unfair everything is

Slam your bedroom door

*or*

Remember that life is very long — you will be able to stay up late eventually

Focus on all the fun things that will happen tomorrow, then get up early and have an interesting morning

Philosophy has been going on for a very long time all round the world because people have always needed help with shouting and panicking a bit less. They've always needed some help with understanding life and how best to deal with it. Over the years, philosophers have come up with a lot of useful ideas that provide this help. Here, in the rest of this book, are twenty-six of our favourite wise ideas.

# KNOW YOURSELF

It sounds odd to say it, but maybe you don't know yourself very well. Of course you know lots of things about yourself—you know what age you are, the colour of your eyes and what you like to have for lunch—but some things are hard to know. Maybe you've never seen the back of your ears, for instance, and probably you don't know much about your Eustachian tubes either (those are the tubes that go from inside your ears to the back of your nose). These sort of things don't actually matter much, but there are more important things you might not know about yourself, which you should: things about your feelings. It's not just you—everyone has difficulty understanding their feelings.

This is because of a funny thing about the way your brain (and everyone else's) works: your brain is very good at noticing that you have a feeling. You know perfectly well that you feel upset or worried or excited. But your brain is not so good at seeing why you feel that feeling. It doesn't automatically remember what is upsetting or worrying you, or what you are really excited about.

Suppose you had planned to bake biscuits with your mum after school. You'd been looking forward to it all day, but then she rings and tells you that something's come up at work, and she won't have time to make the biscuits with you after all. You're disappointed—you don't know what to do now, and everything seems a bit boring. Later, when your mum comes home, you have a feeling that for some reason she is very annoying today. She asks you to clear the table for dinner and instead of getting on with it you shout, 'No!', to which she responds, 'Don't speak to me like that!' Suddenly before you know it, you've stormed out of the kitchen, shouting 'I hate you, you're so bossy!'

You have a big, powerful feeling: 'I am very upset!' but your brain gets confused about what started the feeling. It forgets *why* you are really upset. It's not that you hate your mum, you are just hurt because you really wanted to have a nice time with her and are feeling very disappointed. You don't really think that she is bossy, you are upset that someone you love was too busy to pay you attention earlier. There's a big difference between feeling 'my mum is so bossy', and feeling 'I wish my mum had more time to bake biscuits with me'. But your brain is not very good at seeing the difference.

Imagine this time that you wanted to play football with your older sister. You ask her if she wants to play, but she says she is tired and can't be bothered right now. You go to your room and try to read a book, but it's not very interesting. You wander about the house looking for something to do. Then maybe you see your little brother making a pile of bricks on the floor and you suddenly become angry. You kick the bricks over and he starts to cry. Your brain knows that you're annoyed, but it is not very good at keeping track of what has made you feel that way. Instead of remembering that your sister upset you, your brain thinks it is your

brother and his bricks that you are cross with instead. These are times when you don't know yourself very well. Not knowing yourself causes problems. The more you tell your mum she's bossy, the less likely she is to make biscuits with you (which is what you really want); getting mad with your little brother doesn't get you any closer to playing football with your sister.

But this does not have to be the end of the story. You can get better at knowing yourself. The best way to do this is by asking yourself questions about what you feel. You can ask: what happened earlier that bothered me? Where has my upset come from—maybe not in the last three seconds, but earlier today, or even yesterday?

Imagine that a feeling is a bit like a long, long snake hanging down from a branch of a tree. From where you're standing you can see the snake's head and its forked tongue: that's the feeling of being upset. But you can't see the tail, and the tail is the real reason you feel upset. What branch is the tail curled round? Is it the bossy branch or the biscuit branch; is it the little brother branch or the football branch? You have to find out. You're trying to join up the angry head of the snake with the tail. So, when you are upset you can ask: where is the tail of this feeling? What branch is it hanging from?

A big part of philosophy is asking yourself why you feel what you do: why am I upset? What's really been bothering me? Who has upset me? This isn't just something children can do—it's something a lot of adults should spend a bit more time on as well. Because the better you know your feelings, the more easily you can explain what you're going through.

# An Idea From Socrates

The big, important idea that we have just looked at (that we don't know ourselves very well) comes from a man called Socrates. Socrates lived in the city of Athens in Greece more than two thousand years ago. He wore long robes (like everyone else in those days) and had a long beard—which was probably rather smelly because he was so busy thinking that he often forgot to have a bath.

He liked to walk about the city, meet his friends and ask them questions about what they were excited or worried or puzzled about. His idea was that often people do not know why they have the thoughts and feelings they do. Socrates invented philosophy to help us understand ourselves better. Socrates was very keen on the word 'why'. He was always asking people tricky 'why' questions: why are you friends with this person? Why don't you like so-and-so? He was not being mean or awkward; he really wanted to have an interesting discussion. He wanted to become people's 'thinking-friend'.

You can be like Socrates, too, by being your own thinking-friend. All you have to do is ask yourself questions about what you're feeling—why am I upset with mum? Or, why do I feel like kicking over my little brother's bricks? When you do this you are doing something very special. You are joining in the big conversation of philosophy that's been going on ever since Socrates sat down and started chatting with his friends in Athens.

# LEARN TO SAY WHAT'S ON YOUR MIND

Thanks to Socrates, our thinking-friend from Ancient Greece, we've learnt about how you can get to know yourself better. However, quite often the situation is a bit different: you might know yourself quite well, but what you really wish is that other people understood you better.

The strange and important thing about being you, is that only you know what you are thinking and feeling. Other people cannot automatically understand what's going on inside your head—and they never will, unless you try hard to explain it, normally using quite a few words. They can't guess what you're thinking or how you feel, even though sometimes we all wish that they could, and even imagine that they do.

Your mind is like a box, with all your thoughts and feelings inside it. You can see what's in the box and feel it straight away, but no one else has such immediate access. Your thoughts and feelings are as invisible to other people as they are clear to you. That means there's a big danger:

other people may not understand you, but you will be thinking that they do—or at least that they should.

It's not that other people are mean or stupid when they don't understand what's going on inside your head (even though that's how it sometimes feels). It's just they need to be told—and you need to tell them. It can be really difficult and tiring to do that, but it needs to be done.

When you were a baby, grown-ups could easily guess what was in your 'mind-box'. There were only ever a few simple things you might need from other people. Maybe you were hungry or sleepy or wanted to play a game. At that time, you did not need to explain. Kind people guessed for you, and most of the time they got it right.

Being a baby and having people guess what you were thinking or feeling was nice. But as you get older, it creates a problem: if you are used to kind people being able to guess what's in your head, then you automatically think that it will always be this way—if people are nice and kind, they should be able to guess the contents of your mind. However, as you get older, the thoughts and feelings in your mind have become a lot more complicated than they used to be. You don't just feel tired, or hungry, or like you need to go to the toilet. Now you have thoughts about all different kinds of things. That means that other people can't usually guess what you are truly thinking and feeling.

Suppose you have to go to a party but you really don't want to. You know there will be a boy there that you do not like. He's unfriendly, and you heard him say something horrible about one of your friends. Your mum keeps telling you to hurry up or you'll be late, but you don't want to get ready and you don't want to go at all. She asks if you're not feeling well and you almost say yes, but that's not the real reason. Your mum is trying to be patient but you can tell she wants to go soon. Next, she asks you if you are upset about your shoes, or if you are wearing something you don't like, and you feel like she's such an idiot for getting it so wrong.

All of this happens because sometimes it's easy to forget to use words, or to be scared or embarrassed to use them. You want a grown-up to guess what you're thinking, just like they did when you were a baby. You get angry, annoyed and frustrated that they don't know already. You feel they are being stupid or horrible if they don't guess right. You forget that it's not their fault that they don't know—it's just that they can't see what's in your mind.

Sometimes you might not want to tell someone what is in your mind because it can feel a bit weird. Maybe you do not want to go swimming because you don't like other people seeing your body (even though you used to love swimming), or you do not want to visit your grandparents because you do not like your granny very much (even though you think people are supposed to like their grannies). It can feel like these sorts of things will sound very odd if you say them out loud to someone else. But if you do try to put these feelings into words, your parents might actually understand quite well. They were young once and they have had lots of complicated experiences in their lives, too.

When you don't explain how you feel to other people, it makes you feel like you can't escape. You feel like no one understands you, and that you are all alone. Sometimes all you want to do is sit in your room and cry. But when you try to tell people what's in your mind, it gets better. They mightn't be able to do exactly what you want, or even solve your problem completely, but they will start to understand what you're thinking, and you won't feel so lonely. Knowing someone gets what's going on inside your head feels really nice, and sometimes sharing your problem can be almost as good as getting what you want.

# An Idea from Ludwig Wittgenstein

The questions of how we can get other people to understand what is on our minds was something that really excited a philosopher called Ludwig Wittgenstein. He lived in the first half of the 20th century, from 1889 to 1951. He was German but for a lot of his life he lived and worked in other places—mainly England. His favourite meal was bread and cheese and he loved going to the cinema and flying kites. He was very rich but he did a lot of jobs: he cleaned hospitals, he taught in a school, he was a gardener for a while and he also taught students at university—he even designed a lovely house for his sister in Vienna. He always wanted to build an aeroplane, too, but he never did.

Wittgenstein liked spending time on his own, and he had a little hut in the countryside in Norway where he could go to be by himself and think. He was very interested in what we can do with words. Sometimes, he said, we make pictures with words, so that other people can see what we are thinking about. Imagine you said: 'I saw an interesting dog today'. People don't know what the dog was like just from that, so instead you can give more details: it had long floppy ears, a very short tail and only three legs. Describing words like these help other people to make a picture in their head that's like the picture in your head. Wittgenstein said that when people don't understand one another it's because the pictures in their heads aren't similar enough. When someone doesn't understand something that seems clear in your head, instead of getting frustrated, try to describe it more carefully and see if it helps.

# IT'S HARD TO KNOW WHAT
# WE REALLY WANT

There are all sorts of lovely things that can happen in your life. People are always looking forward to things that are going to happen, or making plans to do things that will make them happy. However, even if you hope something is going to happen that you think will make you happy, often once it does happen, you realise that you don't feel as happy as you had expected! This happens to grown-ups quite a lot.

Maybe at one point you really wanted a frisbee. You saw other people playing with one and it looked great. But, when you got one, you only used it for a few minutes before you realised that actually you didn't really like it and it wasn't that fun. Or perhaps you really wanted to paint the walls of your room your favourite colour—bright yellow or turquoise. It seemed like a great idea, but after you actually did it, it turned out to look horrible and you wished you had never painted it in the first place.

When things like this happen, and something does not make you feel the way you thought it would, it does not mean that there isn't anything that really will make you happy. It just shows that (like everyone) you sometimes find it hard to know in advance what will actually be very nice in reality.

But why does it happen? And how can you get things to turn out better? The big idea here is that you have to start to ask a lot more questions about the things you think you want. Rather than just waiting and hoping to get something, you have to stop and wonder whether it's truly the right thing to be wishing for. As ever, philosophy means asking 'why?' and not giving up until you're sure of the answer—or as sure as you can be.

There are some things that make it tricky to find out what you really want. One of those things is that everybody changes. Even just during the last year, you've probably changed quite a lot, so the things you really wanted then might not be so interesting to you now. But the thing is, your brain doesn't always keep up. It may not have noticed properly that you've been growing, so it might make you think that you still want some of the same things, even though if you got them now, they'd be boring, or wouldn't make you as happy as they might have done before.

Another reason why knowing what you want can be difficult is that things can sound great when you hear about them, but not actually be that nice when you actually do them or have them. It probably sounds really cool to sleep in an igloo, but in reality it would probably just be very damp and cold and a bit creepy.

However, the biggest reason we make the wrong choices is that we are usually very influenced by what other people think. Maybe your friends are all saying that water parks are great, but actually you don't like them.

That does not mean you're strange, or that you should force yourself to like them, and pretend you want to go. The truth is that you are not exactly the same as your friends, and they are not the same as you, so what makes them happy might not be enjoyable for you.

It sounds a bit odd at first, but deciding what you want for your birthday or for Christmas is a philosophical question. You should take time over it. The question, 'What do I really want?' is a huge, important issue—and big, important things take time to answer. It is not just children and teenagers who find it difficult to work out what they really want. Grown-ups have this problem all their lives too. Children and adults are not as different as they sometimes seem.

Adverts are always encouraging us to think that we want more things, and trying to tell us that we will be happy if we buy them. For example, an advert might show a picture of someone with a very expensive new watch looking really happy. This makes our brain think: 'If I get that watch I'll feel as good as the person in the advert.' Maybe it really is a great watch, but the problem is that feeling happy is not actually connected to having a great watch. It is much more about things

like getting on well with your friends, enjoying school or your work, and getting plenty of rest and enough exercise. The watch itself can't make a big difference. We really want something, because we want to feel good about ourselves. But things cannot make us happy, it's experiences and relationships that do that. We might think that a watch or a new pair of shoes is the answer, but it isn't really. The same thing happens with cars, handbags, private jets, new phones or even going to a fancy restaurant. It's weird to think how much of this goes on in the world.

# AN IDEA FROM SIMONE DE BEAUVOIR

A philosopher who was very interested as to why it's hard to know what we really want was a French woman called Simone de Beauvoir. She was born in Paris in 1908, when the very first cars were being made, and died in 1986, by which time nearly everyone had a car. She liked parties and wearing nice clothes, and loved travelling. She wrote many books during her life, and was very good friends with another philosopher who we'll be meeting later—Jean-Paul Sartre (see page 104). They ate lunch together nearly every day, and would talk about the books that they were writing. De Beauvoir had lots of friends and often included them in her books (which sometimes annoyed them). She thought about how easily we stop focusing on what we *really* want and instead go along with what other people seem to want. She realised that we're so aware of other people's opinions that we forget to properly ask ourselves what we really like. She thought that finding out what you really want was the most important job in your life.

De Beauvoir loved to shop, but she wasn't interested in things just because they were expensive or fancy. In fact, she was especially keen on cheap shops. When she was in New York to give talks she loved going to 'dime' shops where everything cost just ten cents. De Beauvoir thought that what we really want is to enjoy our lives, but we make the mistake of thinking that the objects we buy are key to our enjoyment. However, most of the time what matters much more is whether we feel like we have enough time and the freedom to do things we like.

Remember this when you're thinking about what you want. Ask yourself if you really want it, or whether you just think you do. Keep in mind that even if you don't get exactly what you want, it might not have been the thing that would make you happy after all.

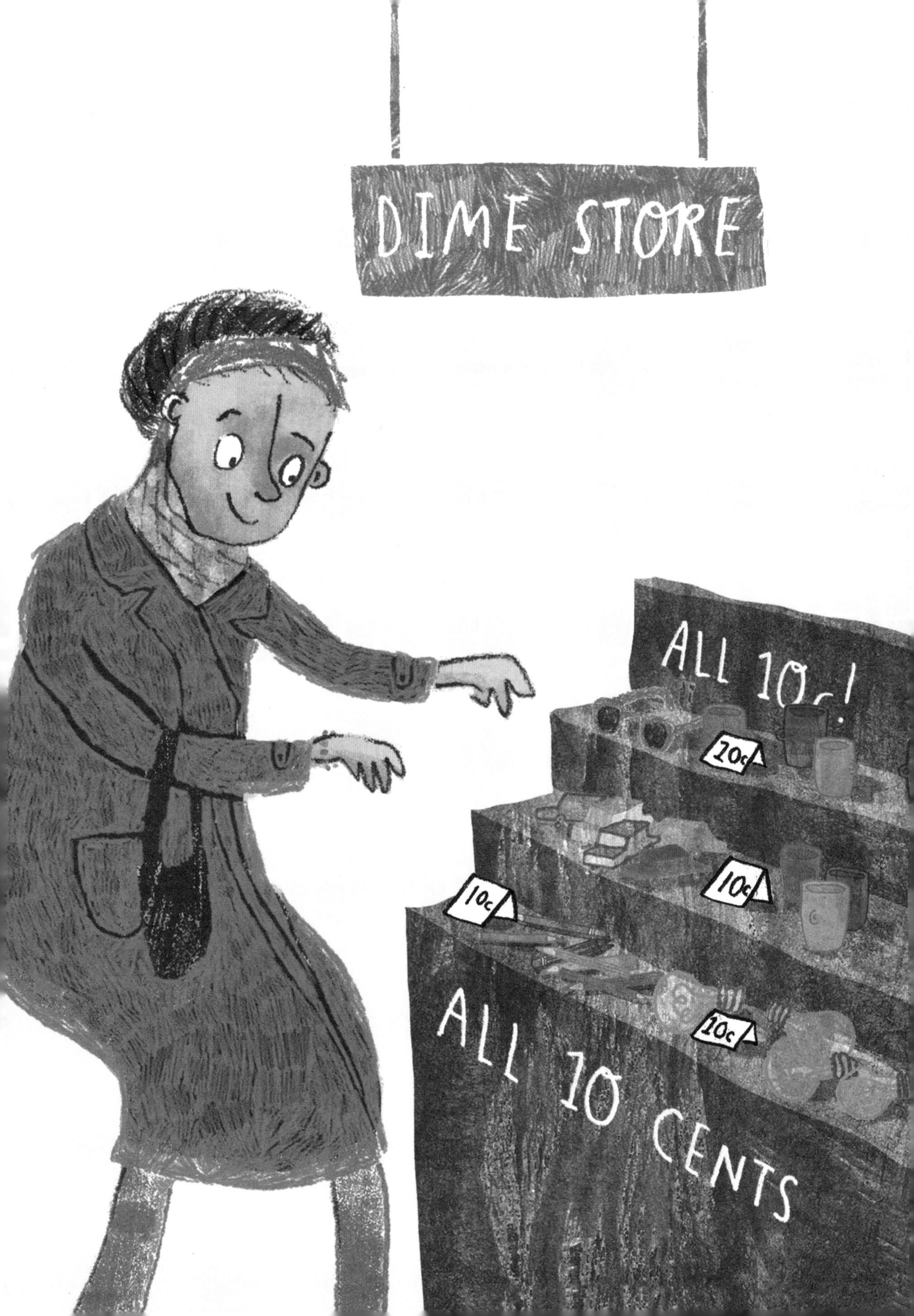
DIME STORE
ALL 10¢!
20¢
10¢
10¢
10¢
ALL 10 CENTS

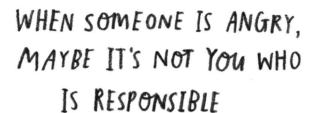

# WHEN SOMEONE IS ANGRY, MAYBE IT'S NOT YOU WHO IS RESPONSIBLE

It is horrible when people (especially parents) get grumpy or annoyed. Sometimes they slam doors or shout, or growl when someone speaks to them. When people act this way, it can feel like it's you they're cross with, and that makes you feel bad—and it can seem unfair as well. But, even though it seems like it, maybe it's not really you they are upset with.

There's an old story called *Androcles and the Lion*, which is set in Ancient Egypt. In the story, a lion comes prowling round a village at night, roaring terribly so that everyone is very frightened. They think the lion is angry with them. Then one day, a man called Androcles is walking out in the countryside and it starts to rain. He takes shelter in a cave—where the lion lives. Androcles thinks the lion is going to eat him, but then he sees that it has a thorn in its paw. The lion didn't really hate the people in the village. It was roaring so much because the thorn hurt, but they didn't realise.

The story is saying something interesting. Angry people (like the angry lion) are usually bothered about something that you can't see. There is often a thorn in there somewhere.

It's a very strange and interesting thought: we feel like we know people very well, but actually we only know a little bit about each other's lives. There's a lot we don't see. Your parents don't really know what it's been like for you all day at school—there are probably lots of things that you never get around to telling them. It's the same for them. They seem big and strong at home and you know them so well in some ways, but it is possible that difficult things happen to them during the day when you are not there.

Androcles, in the story, was unusual: he actually got to see the thorn in the lion's paw, so he realised why the lion was so bad tempered. But most of the time you have to imagine the things that might be hurting other people—the things you can't see or know. Maybe your mum or dad had a difficult meeting at work, or they were very busy all day and are really tired. They're grumpy because of that, not because of you. The meeting or the busy day is like the thorn in the lion's paw. Because you weren't with them at work or at home during the day, you might not know about the reason why they're feeling cross, so you feel it's you they are annoyed with. But probably it has nothing to do with you at all.

It's important for all of us to keep thinking about the thorns we can't see. Don't get upset because someone is in a bad mood or snapped at you—instead, try to imagine what might be the problem, and find a way to help.

# AN IDEA FROM IBN SINA

Plenty of philosophers have been interested in how easy it is for us to misunderstand other people—including thinking they're angry with us when it is really something else that is bothering them. One of the most important was a man called Ibn Sina, who is sometimes called Avicenna.

Ibn Sina was born about a thousand years ago and lived most of his life in Iran (which was called Persia at that time). He was a scientist and a very successful doctor, and a lot of princes and rulers wanted him to be their adviser. Sina was a devout Muslim, but he was very curious about all different kinds of ideas and religions, and spent a lot of time studying two Greek philosophers in this book, Socrates and Aristotle. Ibn Sina worked extremely hard. He often stayed up late to read and write and study.

Ibn Sina thought that everyone has two parts to them: an outside part, which everyone can see, and an inside part (he called it the 'soul'), which only they know. We learn about other people from what they do and say, but often we don't see enough of them to get a true picture of what they are really like. It is amazing that someone who lived so long ago had such good and useful ideas about why you might not properly understand people—and why you might think they are annoyed with you, when really they are upset about something completely different. That thing might be something that you can't see, but it's something you can learn to imagine.

# PEOPLE ARE UNHAPPY, NOT MEAN

Some children aren't very nice to their brothers and sisters, or to their classmates at school. They call them names, pick on them or try to spoil their fun. They might pretend to be your friend and then say very unkind things behind your back. It seems like all they want is for other people to feel small and stupid. It can be really upsetting and frightening to be on the receiving end of this kind of bullying. But why are people mean? Why does one person want to make another person feel miserable?

The answer is very surprising: it is because they feel small and miserable inside of themselves. You wouldn't know by looking at them—they might look strong and confident and very pleased with themselves. They might seem to laugh a lot—maybe at you.

But if you think about it, no one who was really happy would want to make another person unhappy. People who are actually strong and confident are almost always gentle and kind to others. If someone is mean and a bully it is because at home, or in the past, something or someone has frightened them a lot. Probably you'll never know the details, but you can imagine. Maybe they have an older brother who picks on them. Maybe their mum is always bossing them about. Maybe their parents shout at each other. Inside their head, this person who seems so brave and fearless, actually feels sad and worried. They're too frightened to let anyone see how weak they really feel, so they try to make themselves feel better by making another person suffer.

Those who have been hurt, hurt others. Understanding this does not immediately solve the problem if someone is being nasty to you, but it can still help a little. It can help you to remember that you don't deserve to be treated badly, that it's not something you've done and that there isn't anything wrong with you. The best way to understand a bully or a mean person is to put yourself in their position. Think about a time when you haven't been very nice to someone. Most people are a bit mean to someone at some point, or have at least wanted to be horrible, even if they don't actually do or say anything. It's not bad or wrong, it's just life. Now think about why you were mean to that person—it's pretty much always because something else was bothering you that you didn't know how to put right.

For instance, it is quite common for older children to get a bit nasty if there is a new baby in the family. Grown-ups think babies are very sweet. Everyone pays them attention and says how lovely they are, and parents spend all their time looking after them. If you are a bit older and your parents have a new baby, it is not surprising if you get cross. You might feel like people should be paying more attention to you. Maybe you want to show other people that you're also important—that in fact you are much better than this boring baby who everyone loves so much. So you find someone who is weaker than you, and a bit babyish, and you start being mean to them. It makes you feel powerful, and it makes you feel better to know that someone else is feeling bad like you do. Of course, doing this isn't very nice at all, but it is understandable. Sometimes when we are so sad and angry, there doesn't feel like anything else we can do. Realising why you might not be very nice to other people sometimes will help you to see how someone else could be not very nice to you.

Understanding doesn't make everything suddenly perfect. If someone is bullying you or hurting you, the problem will not go away just because you are able to understand that they must be very unhappy inside. Philosophy does not solve all your problems in one go. But when you understand things they stop being so frightening. And that's a good start.

# MEANNESS AND UNHAPPINESS

*Write down a list of the people who are mean to you. Then write why you think*
*they might be unhappy. How might their meanness and unhappiness be related?*

| PERSON WHO IS BEING MEAN | REASONS WHY THEY MIGHT BE UNHAPPY |
| --- | --- |
| | |

# AN IDEA FROM ZERA YACOB

One philosopher who thought a lot about why people are mean to each other was Zera Yacob. He was born in Ethiopia in Africa, around four hundred years ago, in 1599. His parents were poor and he was brought up on a small farm, but when he grew up he became a teacher.

At that time Ethiopia was split into different religious groups who were bitterly opposed to each other, but Zera Yacob didn't want to take sides. Some people told lies about him to the king and he had to go into hiding. For two years he lived on his own in a cave. That might sound pretty awful, but he rather liked spending time alone and he said he learned more by thinking in his cave than he had when he was at school. Eventually a new king came to power and Zera Yacob could leave his cave and go to live in a town. He found work teaching the children of a rich businessman—he was a very good teacher and the family were kind to him. Later he got married and had a family.

Zera Yacob thought that life is always quite difficult for everyone. Everyone suffers. That's a sad thought, and it should make us kind and sympathetic to each other. But some people become mean and cruel by mistake. They think that if they hurt others it will take away their own pain. Zera Yacob believed that if we can admit our own sadness it will make us less angry with other people—and the amount of pain in the world will decrease.

# DON'T EXPECT TOO MUCH

Imagine that you are really looking forward to something. Maybe it's your birthday soon, or you're going on holiday. You start to imagine how nice it will be. Everything will be wonderful. You will get all the presents you want, or you'll be able to swim at the beach every day. Everyone will be happy, and nothing will go wrong. But, when it really is your birthday or you really do go on holiday, something is not right. You get some nice presents, but some boring ones you didn't want, too. On holiday you do get to swim, but not every day: one day you have to go to an art gallery with your mum, and on another day it rains non-stop. Your parents get annoyed when you keep asking, 'Can we go to the beach now?' You feel grumpy and irritated. You are disappointed. You thought it was all going to be so great—and now it isn't. But the funny thing is, your birthday and the holiday were not really terrible at all. They were pretty good. It's just that they weren't as good as you'd imagined.

Sometimes it also works the other way round. You might imagine that something is going to be horrible. Maybe you're getting a new teacher and you've heard that they're really nasty. Apparently they shout a lot and never let you do anything interesting or fun. But when the new teacher arrives, they turn out to be quite a lot nicer than you had been expecting. They do shout a little, but they are kind of funny as well. They are quite strict, but they also teach you how to be better at art and let you do some fun science experiments. You'd been expecting them to be horrible, so it's a nice surprise when they're not that bad after all. Either way, whether you get grumpy or feel pleased about something depends a lot on your expectations. If you expect things to be perfect, it's no surprise that you might be disappointed. If you expect things to be bad, you quite often get a nice surprise.

There is a good trick you can play to make sure you are nicely surprised more often than you are disappointed. If you try not to get your hopes up too much, then usually things will turn out better than you expected. You'll be especially pleased, without really having to do anything at all. And even if it is a little disappointing, remember: it could always be a bit worse. Don't worry though—imagining things going badly doesn't make anything bad happen. If you imagine getting a lump of coal for a birthday present it doesn't mean anyone will actually give you one. If you imagine missing the bus in the morning it does not mean you will miss it. How you imagine things in the future doesn't make them happen. But it does something else: it protects and prepares you against sadness when things do (sometimes) go wrong.

The way you imagine the future can make the difference between getting furious whenever something goes worse than you thought it would, and getting a nice surprise whenever something is a bit nicer than you had expected. Expecting less is a big part of what it means to be a philosopher.

# AN IDEA FROM SENECA

There once was a philosopher who lived a long time ago in Ancient Rome who spent a lot of time thinking about why people get angry. His name was Seneca. Seneca was a businessman and a politician; however he was also an important philosopher (sometimes we forget that you can be a philosopher as well as being other things, too).

At one point, Seneca was given the most difficult job in the world—he was appointed tutor to a really terrifying young man called Nero, who later became emperor. If Nero got angry because someone didn't laugh at one of his jokes, it wasn't unusual for him to stab the other person or throw them in prison. Seneca realised that the problem with Emperor Nero was that his expectations were too high. Nero expected everything to be perfect and constantly lost his temper when it wasn't.

Seneca told him that getting angry and upset was caused by optimism. Optimism means thinking that things are always going to go very well and exactly as you want. Instead of being an optimist, Seneca thought that the best way to stay calm and be happier was to become a pessimist. That is, someone who assumes that things will probably turn out quite badly and generally has a negative view of the future. It's an interesting and strange idea: that maybe our happiness does not depend on what actually happens, but on our expectations. Pessimists can sometimes be happier than optimists, because pessimists are always discovering that things are much nicer and better than they thought they would be.

# MAYBE YOU ARE JUST TIRED

When you are in a bad mood, you usually want to blame someone. You feel fed up and annoyed and your brain looks around to see whose fault it could be—your teacher, your parents, your friends, maybe your brother or sister. But sometimes it's not really anyone's fault. Instead, there's a very different kind of explanation. Nothing is really wrong at all, you are just feeling grumpy and bothered because you haven't been getting enough sleep and you are tired.

Imagine you are running and you come to a hill. If you have just started running and you've got lots of energy, the hill isn't a problem. You don't mind. It will be fun to see how fast you can run up it. But if you've been running for quite a long way already and your legs ache and you're out of breath, the hill will seem horrible. You can't face it. It's exactly the same hill but you feel very differently about it—and it all depends on how tired you are. It is the same with lots of things, and not only physical things either. Maybe you have to do quite a difficult maths sum. If you're feeling full of energy, you don't mind. It's tricky but you can have a go. But if you are very tired, it feels too hard. It makes you angry and upset that you have to do it. It's the same sum. The difference is that you're tired.

Being told that 'maybe you are just tired' can be really irritating. Usually it doesn't feel like that's the reason why you are in bad mood. The trouble is that you can be tired but not notice. Once again, your brain doesn't realise what's really going on.

It is not only being tired that can put you in a bad mood. It could also be that you are hungry, or haven't drunk enough water, or you have spent too much time indoors and have not been running around enough. It could even be that winter has been going on too long and you haven't had enough sunshine. All these things make a difference to the mood you are in.

We don't usually think about these things when we're in a bad mood, and instead, we imagine that the reason we feel upset is because of something someone else has done. We get so wound up that we want to shout at them and tell them how horrid they are. But what will actually make us feel better might be a rest, a glass of water, some lunch or a play outside. It is odd—but interesting—that you can forget there might be very simple reasons you're feeling upset. The good thing about simple reasons, though, is that they can be fixed simply, too. It isn't that easy to make up with a friend after an argument, get your mum to be less busy with work or suddenly to become brilliant at singing or basketball—but you can get a glass of water. You can't make that bully at school like you, but you can eat a sandwich.

Adults are especially bad at seeing that they might be in a bad mood just because they are tired. Adults like to think that if they feel upset it must be for a big, important reason—probably something to do with politics or world affairs, or because their boss at work is much more stupid than they could ever be. It's hard for them to remember that a bad feeling can have a very simple explanation: maybe they just stayed up too late last night or should urgently have some orange juice.

# A CHECKLIST TO SEE IF I'M JUST TIRED

*When you suddenly feel sad, before you despair, see if the following might apply:*

○ I have not had anything to eat for a few hours

○ I went to bed very late last night

○ I had a really busy day at school today

*Add in a few other 'small' explanations for feeling like you have very big problems:*

○ _____

○ _____

○ _____

○ _____

# AN IDEA FROM MATSUO BASHO

The philosopher Matsuo Basho was interested in the way that small, simple things can make a big difference to our lives. He lived in Japan over three hundred years ago. He came from a very ordinary family and when he was quite young he worked as a servant in the house of a local nobleman, who was a very good employer and helped a lot with Matsuo's education. When he was older he lived on his own in a small hut and went for long walks in the countryside. He had a career as a poet, writing very, very short poems called haikus. They were extremely popular, so he was able to make quite a lot of money. But Basho didn't want to live a fancy life. He was very fond of nature, particularly liking trees and flowers, and he loved watching frogs in a nearby pond. Matsuo Basho thought that we often get bothered and upset because we forget about simple things. We think that it must only be big, complicated things that are important.

Matsuo Basho liked to tell people how much he enjoyed little things: having a cup of tea in the morning, eating simple vegetables on a winter's day (he recommended leeks), listening to a bird chirping away, looking at clouds or watching raindrops. He was an important philosopher who reminds people, even today, of the strange fact that our mood, and our feeling of whether life is pleasing or horrible, can depend on such tiny things. They seem so small, but they make a big difference to us.

# WHAT IS NORMAL ISN'T NORMAL

When people say hurtful things to each other, they often use the insult that someone isn't 'normal'. They call them crazy, weird or a freak—there are lots of different ways of saying it, but they're all trying to suggest that someone is bad for being *different*.

The thing is, people don't really know very much about what is normal. Everyone has an idea of 'normal', but it's probably very much mistaken. Maybe in one group of friends it's normal to be into cars or a particular pop group, but that is only normal among that small group of people — and it is likely that not all of them are really that interested anyway, they might simply pretend to fit in with what they think everyone else likes. In another group of friends it might be normal to like completely different things.

What seems normal can change a lot as well. It used to be normal that children didn't go to school—instead, most of them stayed at home and worked with their parents, usually on a farm. They would think it was very strange to sit in a classroom and learn about the world. But even today, what's normal in one school might be strange in another one. At school in Japan the children chat together about their pet robot dogs, but probably if you did that people would think you were weird. If people think you're not quite normal, you might just be a bit unlucky—maybe the things you like are not very popular in the corner of the world you happen to live in right now, but they wouldn't seem at all strange if you lived somewhere else, or at a different time.

In fact, it is normal to be quite weird. At first that sounds crazy. How can it be normal to be strange? But it makes sense when you think about it. What 'normal' means is 'like other people'. But what are other people really like? It is much trickier to answer this question than you might suppose. As we've already discovered earlier in this book, you don't get to see the whole of anyone. Everyone is much more strange and interesting than they may seem: they have weird thoughts in the middle of the night that they never tell other people about. When they're on their own they do funny things that they would never do in front of other people. They act completely differently, too, when they are with their granny or their mum than the way they do at school with their friends. That's because the way someone is at school is only a little part of who they really are. You know this, because that's what you are like. Other children at school are really much more unusual than they appear. If you feel odd or weird sometimes, don't worry—you probably have a lot more in common with others than you think. It is just that the others are keeping the odder bits of themselves hidden.

You might think: 'I do not care about being normal. What is so good about being normal anyway?' It's a good question. A lot of philosophers started to have good ideas when they stopped caring so much about what others thought. Maybe you will, too.

# AN IDEA FROM ALBERT CAMUS

Albert Camus was a French philosopher who was born in Algeria in 1913. At that time, Algeria was part of France. His parents were very poor—his father worked on a farm and his mother was a cleaner. However, the local school was very good and he got an excellent education. He loved going to the beach and was very talented at football—he was a goalkeeper and the team he played for was hugely successful. He felt that he learned more about philosophy from playing football than from all the books he read.

When he was older, Camus moved to Paris. He worked as a newspaper journalist and liked going to cafés. Camus was interested in the strange feelings that go on inside people—especially when they are excited or sad. One of his biggest aims was to convince people to worry a bit less about how other people judge them. Doing this yourself can make you feel less worried, less lonely, and give you the confidence to explore new things.

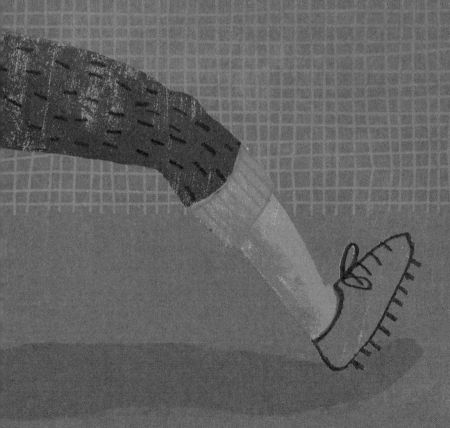

# NO ONE KNOWS...

In lots of ways, adults can seem very impressive. They may seem to have all the answers, but there is a big secret about them: they do not know everything. Usually an adult only knows about a few things. One adult might know a lot about trees or engines, but know very little about how a phone really works or the history of the kings and queens of England. Another might know a lot about books or electricity, but very little about Antarctica or sports.

In fact, there are lots and lots of things—even important things—that absolutely no one knows. No one really understands how to make cities very nice, for instance. If they did know, all the cities in the world would be beautiful, clean and lovely to live in. But most of them are not. No one knows the very best way to run a school, either—that's why there are lots of schools in the world that aren't very good and why not every teacher is wonderful. This isn't because adults are stupid, but because the problems are so difficult. If you want to see a grown-up looking confused you could ask them what time is. Not 'what is the time?' (they will probably know that!), but what is time itself? That is a difficult question, isn't it? Or, how about asking them why some jokes are funnier than others, or whether a dog knows that it is a dog. We promise you they will not know. Hardly anyone really knows anything about those things.

Adults disagree about a huge range of issues: how should the country be run? What should we do about pollution? Who should get the biggest salaries? You can have conversations about these things, too, and it does not matter if you don't know for sure—because adults don't know either.

Adults do know a lot. But—and it's important to keep reminding yourself of this—they're often very unsure about a lot of really important things in their own lives. They can seem very impressive: they've got a job, they are married to someone and they might own a house and a car. Inside, though, they probably do not really know why they got married to this person (maybe it would have been better with someone else), they wonder if they should be doing a different job and they worry about paying the bills. Perhaps they don't know whether they should ask for a promotion at work or where it would be good to go on holiday. They feel they have to make a lot of big decisions but they don't know if they're making the right ones. That's why they often look very serious, and sometimes get snappy.

One day, you will be an adult too. It might seem quite a long way off now, but the strange thing is that you won't feel so very different from the way you do at the moment. You'll still be you, even though you'll have a job, will have learnt to drive a car and might even have children of your own. You will have done all these huge things, but there'll still be lots of things you don't know—and that you may never know.

It is good to have a little part of your brain that constantly keeps in mind that there are lots of important things that adults don't know. This does not mean that adults are stupid (even though it is quite nice to imagine they have thinking problems, too), it just means that they are the same as everyone else. Remembering that adults do not know everything can make some of them a little less frightening. It makes you feel a bit sorry for them, and it helps you to see that you are not so different, and that your ideas are, at points, just as important as theirs. We can actually be quite nice to each other when we realise that we're all faced with similar problems. And we can all have a go at thinking—which is what ends up making the whole world cleverer.

# THINGS I WOULD LIKE TO KNOW MORE ABOUT

*Make a list of things you would like to find out more about. For example:*

○   How much do animals really understand?

○   Why do we dream?

○   Is there life on other planets?

○   Is the internet bad or good?

○   _____

○   _____

○   _____

○   _____

# An Idea from René Descartes

René Descartes was a French philosopher who was born in 1596 and lived most of his life in Paris and Amsterdam. He had a little pointed beard and often wore a large black hat. He was very good at maths, but he also spent quite a few years as a soldier. What he liked best was thinking. He often used to stay in bed all morning just to think. His friends thought he was very lazy—though actually he wasn't at all, because thinking is hard work. On one extremely cold day he sat in a large oven (it wasn't very hot at the time) and thought about how little anyone really knows for sure. He was amazed by how much people think they know, but don't really. What people don't realise is how so much of what they believe is fact is really just an opinion. And opinions can quite easily be wrong.

Descartes was very good at feeling puzzled. He thought that being clever meant being able to think and wonder about a lot of things. One thing that really puzzled him was whether a dog can think for itself. Does a dog think about how far away the moon is, or ask itself a question? He was also very puzzled by the difference between a thought and a physical thing. You can say that your finger is 6.5cm long, and you can measure it to see whether that is true. But you can't use a ruler to measure an idea. Descartes never quite worked out a good answer to these puzzles—but he became famous for asking interesting questions.

Descartes also liked how the idea of the ignorance of other people could make him feel more confident. People act as if they know all kinds of things, but they don't really. They seem to know exactly how everything should work, what a good job is, what you should do with your free time, what's the right way to run a country, who should be in charge and what should be taught in schools.

But actually people don't know the best answers to these things. They aren't stupid—it's just that the questions are so hard we haven't worked out the right answers yet. Everyone has the opportunity to be a thinker.

# POLITENESS MATTERS

It can seem quite boring to have to be polite. There's probably some times that your mum or dad comes into your room and asks, 'How'd you get on today?' but you don't feel much like answering. It's not a very interesting question. Maybe you are reading a magazine and eating some toast, and you don't even look up. Or maybe your grandparents send you a book for your birthday. It's quite a nice book, but you don't want to send them a thank you letter, or ring them up. You might be busy or maybe you feel a bit shy. Perhaps another time, your dad makes you something really tasty for lunch. You really enjoyed eating it, but why would you need to tell him it was nice? He's your dad. He knows it's nice—he made it!

You like your parents (most of the time), and your grandparents, too, but maybe you don't imagine that it matters much to them if you answer or say thanks or say, 'That was really lovely, thanks for making it.' They're grown-ups and you are just a kid. They can drive a car and have credit cards. It doesn't feel like it could make any difference to them what you say—or don't say.

The funny thing is that, on the inside, grown-ups are not as strong as they seem. They worry and get hurt easily. They worry about love, they worry about their jobs, they worry about you. If you do not answer when your parents ask you about your day, they'll worry that you might be cross with them. If you don't say thank you when they make something for you to eat, they'll worry that they can't please you. Your grandparents want to give you a present you like, and if they don't hear from you, they'll worry that you didn't like it—and more importantly, that you don't like them.

You don't usually realise how unsure grown-ups actually are. You don't realise that you can hurt their feelings with just a few words, or by not saying anything. You can make them feel sad or silly. It's strange to think that you have this power. Grown-ups are much more like you than you might imagine.

It may have seemed to you before that the reason for being polite is that other people are more powerful than you and they will get angry if you are not nice to them. Far from it. Politeness matters because people are fragile and need to be handled with care.

We don't usually mean to hurt people's feelings, but sometimes we just do not realise that we can, or we forget that people get hurt easily. You might not always remember that by not responding to someone you could make them worried or sad. It seems such a little thing—just looking up and saying 'Hi—school was fine,' or, 'I liked the book,' or, 'Thanks for making me lunch, dad.' These aren't little things really, though. They are powerful words that can comfort and bring a smile to the face of anyone, even someone who has been alive on the earth for five times as long as you have.

# AN IDEA FROM CONFUCIUS

One of the philosophers who thought and cared most about politeness lived in China about two-and-a-half thousand years ago. His name was Confucius. His father was a soldier, but sadly he died when Confucius was still very young, and after that the family were quite poor. When he left school, Confucius started a career as a government official and eventually he became an important adviser to the local rulers of different parts of China. Confucius lived at a time when the generals of armies could do what they wanted—they were in charge because they were stronger than anyone else.

Their manners were frequently very bad. They grunted and swore and didn't look at people when they spoke.

Confucius thought that this was a very serious problem. He believed that government had to be good and that an important part of goodness was paying attention to manners and etiquette. He thought a lot about bowing (the Chinese version of our handshakes), and how two people should bow to one another so that neither side would feel offended or hurt in the process. Confucius knew that manners matter, because the wrong words can be—as he put it—as wounding as a sword.

# WHY WE PROCRASTINATE

You might not know the word 'procrastinate', or maybe you've heard it before but are not sure exactly what it means. It's quite an unusual word. However, even if you've never heard it before, you probably do know about the thing that it means. Procrastinate is made from two Latin words: *pro* and *cras*. *Pro* means 'towards' and *cras* means 'tomorrow'. Together they mean 'putting off doing something—until tomorrow, or some other time'. Perhaps you do this sometimes, too. Imagine that you have something you need to do for school: it's a piece of writing about what you did on holiday. It is for quite a scary teacher, so you want to make it very good and, in a way, you're excited about it. It's going to be long and you've been asked to use a dictionary. You've got the whole weekend. On Friday you think, 'I'll do it tomorrow'. On Saturday you think, 'I'll do it on Sunday'. On Sunday you think, 'I'll do it tonight'. But on Sunday evening you realise: it's too late to do it now. Now you're fed up with yourself for procrastinating.

It would be easy to accuse you of being lazy, but it's more complicated than that. We need to find out why we put things off in this way (you're not the only one who does it—almost everyone has this problem). Luckily, one of the useful things about philosophy is that instead of letting you get annoyed with yourself, it can give you some answers as to why you—and other people—have a problem.

The main thing that makes you procrastinate is fear. That sounds odd at first, because you probably don't feel like you are afraid of doing your homework. But maybe in some way you are scared—scared of not doing as well as you want to. You might have a picture in your mind of how good your homework should be, and it makes the idea of it not being as good as you want it to be difficult to think about. The problem is that if you start and it doesn't turn out as well as you would like, the difficult idea might come true. So you put off starting to avoid the fear of disappointment. If you don't start, you can't spoil anything. You can't get anything wrong. People who procrastinate aren't lazy; they are often just perfectionists, who can't bear the pain of not quite getting things right.

The solution to putting work off isn't to get more and more annoyed with yourself. Instead, you have to convince yourself that things are worth doing even if they are a bit wrong. You also need to accept that lots of things are actually much trickier than they look—so you can't always get them right the first time (or maybe even the second or the tenth time). It's not impossible—you just have to keep going. It might feel like other people are better at things than you, but you don't get to see all the practice other people had to do first. They are not just magically good at doing things. They made lots and lots of mistakes. What made them successful is not that they had no problems, but that they kept going.

You will be able to finally get down to work when the fear of maybe not doing something quite as well as you'd like is wiped out by the greater and more serious fear of not doing anything at all.

# AN IDEA FROM HYPATIA OF ALEXANDRIA

Hypatia was a philosopher who lived at the end of the Roman Empire. She died in 405, around the same time as a huge German tribe—the Goths—attacked and captured the city of Rome itself.

Hypatia lived in Alexandria on the Mediterranean coast of Egypt, which was famous for having the tallest lighthouse and the best library in the world. Hypatia taught mathematics and music as well as philosophy. She was very interested in making difficult things easier to understand. Her father was a teacher as well and together they wrote one of the first philosophy books for children (though it had more maths in it than this one, because at that time people did not split up different subjects the way we do).

Hypatia was famous for being a very good teacher—she was an extremely calm and friendly person. She believed in the importance of taking small steps, and was sure that everyone had the ability to learn a lot, eventually. But, she said, we have to start out not knowing things—that's not our fault, it's inevitable. Instead of calling her students lazy, she tried to really understand what they were finding difficult. She thought we get put off from doing difficult things because we haven't been taught how to start with the easiest, simplest steps first. We get scared, and we procrastinate, but, as Hypatia knew, we aren't just lazy.

# WHY IT'S HARD TO KNOW WHAT YOU WANT TO DO WITH YOUR LIFE

Sometimes people ask you the question, 'what do you want to be when you grow up?' You may feel that you are supposed to know. It can be a bit frightening. You know you will have to do something—because everyone does—but how are you supposed to find out what that will be?

Some children and young people feel that they do know: they say they want to be a vet or a football player or a farmer or a dentist. These are very nice ideas, but things do not often work out quite the way you expect when you were younger. Actually, it is quite hard to figure out what you should do when you are older—and it is totally understandable that it might take a long time to find a good answer.

One confusing thing is that some kinds of job (just a very small number) are famous, so you hear about them a lot. But these jobs are famous because they're special in some way, and that usually means that hardly anyone gets to do them. Hardly anyone becomes a successful actor, or develops games or invents something and becomes very rich. Very few people work as a model or become a sports star, either. And actually, these jobs might not be very nice. Famous people don't usually enjoy being famous, because if you are famous a lot of other people who do not really know you criticise you and say mean things about you because they are jealous. It does not look this way from the outside, and it is not what the media portrays, but it's the truth. Fortunately, there are lots of interesting jobs you can do that you might not hear much about.

So how do you work out what you want to do? A good answer is that you could stop thinking about what might please other people or what might make you money and start to focus on what you really enjoy. Maybe you like organising things, or being creative or solving problems. Maybe you like explaining things to others, or you're interested in how people make food or you like talking about things with other people and hearing what they have to say. It doesn't matter that these things don't (yet) sound like jobs—they are the most important bits of the jobs of your future.

It can seem quite strange to talk about what you 'enjoy' in this context. Enjoyment and fun can sound like the opposite of work, but if you want to be good at something you need to enjoy it. You don't have to know yet what actual job you would like to do, you just have to concentrate on doing constructive things that you like to do, and getting good at them. Work is a strange mixture of having to do what other people want (so you can get paid) and finding things you like spending your time doing (so you can do them well).

One important thing to consider that you might not have thought about is what games you like to play and how you like to play them. This can be really helpful when thinking about what you might want to do when you are older. As we mentioned before, play is not really the opposite of work—in fact, what children do when they are playing is a kind of practice for work. It is not the actual game that counts—but the way you do it. Maybe when you're building stuff with Lego you really enjoy following the instructions—that might mean you'd enjoy working in an office. Or maybe you like sorting out the Lego bricks before you start, putting all the same colours and shapes together so you know where everything is—that might mean you would enjoy a job where you have to be precise and clear about what you're doing, like a pharmacist or an optician. Or perhaps you

like to freestyle and make whatever comes to mind first, never following the instructions—that might mean you'd like being something creative like an art director at an advertising agency, or a graphic designer. These are just a few examples, but they show a pattern: work is more like play than you might at first think. The problem a lot of adults have with their job is that it's not enough like the play they used to enjoy. When they were choosing their jobs they probably didn't think enough about what they liked doing when they were younger—and they are paying a heavy price for it.

## AN IDEA FROM JEAN-JACQUES ROUSSEAU

Jean-Jacques Rousseau was a Swiss philosopher who lived in the 18th century, from 1712 to 1778. His father had a small business making watches in Geneva, and he loved reading to young Jean-Jacques. As he got older, Rousseau liked music and going for long walks on his own. He was very independent. One time, when he was a teenager, he went out walking in the fields around Geneva. When he got back to the city, the gates were shut (in those days many cities were surrounded by walls and at night the gates were closed). Instead of waiting for the morning, he set off on an adventure, and walked all the way to the next country: France. Later in his life, Rousseau became very famous, but he never made much money—that was fine though, because he thought it was nicer to live a simple, ordinary life than to be rich and live in a grand house.

One of Rousseau's big ideas was that children are often more alive inside than adults. He worried that instead of just learning more, adults actually forget the important things they already learnt when they were little. Instead of adults always teaching children, Rousseau thought that they should sometimes try to learn from children. He also said that we should try to find work that suits our own nature. It might sound obvious, but it isn't really, because so often we're guided by what other people think a good job is. Rousseau took children's games very seriously; they were, he said, the first moment when we start to realise what sort of things we might do when we are older.

# GOOD THINGS ARE
# (UNEXPECTEDLY) HARD

Some things are obviously very difficult to do. It would be brilliant to be able to ride a bicycle along a tightrope, but of course it would take years and years of practice and lots of falls and accidents to learn how to do that.

There are other things that look quite easy to do. You might see someone standing up on stage performing comedy—they seem to be very relaxed, just saying whatever comes into their heads. That makes it look as if it would be quite easy to be a comedian, but actually, in order to make it look so easy, they've been practising at home for years. It's quite likely that they stand in front of a mirror and think seriously about whether they should raise one eyebrow while they tell a joke, or keep their left hand in their pocket when they tell another joke. On top of this, they will have failed many times before you see them perform. They will have told jokes that no one found funny, they will have been booed and heckled and told they were no good. You don't see all the practice they have had to do and all the difficulties they have had to face. It may look easy, but actually it is not easy at all.

Lots of things are like this. In fact, almost all the good and interesting things in life are quite hard to do—it is just that people do not usually tell you how hard they are. They would like to be encouraging and so they ignore the difficulties—the ones they have experienced and the ones you might face in the future. When people pretend things aren't hard in this way, they think they're helping you. They worry that if you realise how hard something is, you will give up, or won't give it a go. They are trying to be nice. But in reality, they are creating problems for you later on. By mistake, they're setting you up to be disappointed when you eventually do face something difficult—because instead of being prepared for the difficulties, you thought everything would be relatively easy.

Of course, there are also some things that everyone admits are very tricky, and therefore a lot of time and effort is put into learning how to do them. We all know that it's difficult to learn how to read, for instance. So you get a lot of help with this challenge. Teachers have to go to university to learn about teaching children to read. There are lots of picture books for babies, with just a few words, to help you when you are beginning. No one expects you to learn to read in a few minutes—of course it is going to take a long time and a lot of practice, and you will need a lot of help.

Musical instruments are very hard, too. You have probably looked at a piano or a violin before and thought how fun it would be to be able to play it—then you tried for three minutes and it sounded horrible! It can take three years to get just a simple, nice tune out of a violin, and even more to be really good at it. Lots of things turn out to be like learning to play a musical instrument: strangely and horribly hard.

It's so hard to make a good friend, it's hard to write a story that you like, it's hard to understand your parents sometimes, or to work out what you want to do when you are older. But people don't usually talk about the fact that these things are difficult. In fact, they often make you think that they should be easy, while really they can be as tricky as learning to read or play the violin. They all take a long time and you need—and deserve—a lot of help with doing them. When you understand that things are difficult and will take ages to learn to do properly, you will get less stressed when they go wrong—which sometimes, unfortunately, they will. The big problem is not that certain things are hard, it is that we keep expecting them to be easy.

# THINGS THAT ARE HARD THAT I WOULD LIKE TO LEARN (ONE DAY)

*Make a list of things of things that you would like to learn to do, as well as what you will do with your new skill. For example:*

○  How to speak another country's language...
   and then I'll make friends with someone from there.

○  How to dance with confidence...
   and then I'll ask someone to dance with me.

○  How to ride a bike...
   and then I'll travel somewhere new and exciting.

○  How to... _____

   and then I'll... _____

○  How to... _____

   and then I'll... _____

○  How to... _____

   and then I'll... _____

## AN IDEA FROM FRIEDRICH NIETZSCHE

The philosopher who was most interested in the way that good things are difficult was a man called Friedrich Nietzsche. He was born in 1844, in the middle of the 19th century. He was quite serious when he was little and was very good at schoolwork—though he had mixed feelings about the extremely strict school he went to. He argued a lot with his sister and mother, too. When Nietzsche was older he worked for a while as a teacher at a university, but he wasn't a very good teacher and he was often unwell. So instead of teaching, he decided to travel. He spent a lot of time living in the mountains of Switzerland and grew an enormous moustache. He looked quite fierce but he was very polite and was often cracking jokes. He wrote a lot of books but at first hardly anyone was interested in them, and they sold only a few copies. After he died, however, Nietzsche's books became very famous and lots and lots of people read them.

Nietzsche thought that people are often frightened of doing things that they find difficult—even though those things might be very important. He said that we tell ourselves that we do not really want the difficult things, even though secretly we do. For example, imagine someone who secretly wants to be very good at maths, but they find it really hard. They might tell themselves that maths is stupid and only stupid people care about being good at it. This is a story they tell themselves to hide their secret ambition. Nietzsche would have understood. His ideas remind us that we should admit that things are hard, but do them anyway—knowing that they will get easier the more we try, and that we will get a great reward at the end of our efforts.

# WEAKNESS OF STRENGTH THEORY

If you want to go from New York to Paris, the easiest and fastest way is, of course, to go by aeroplane. There are lots of things about an aeroplane that make it fantastic for travelling long distances—its huge wings, for example, or powerful engine. However, if you think about it, an aeroplane would be just about the worst possible way of trying to get home from school, or going to the shops. Exactly the same things that make a plane great for long distances would make it terrible for driving around in a town or city. The roads would be too narrow for its giant wings, and the engine would probably destroy all of the shop windows. There would certainly be nowhere to park. What this can show us is that the strengths of the plane for flying long distances can also be weaknesses when it comes to a short trip.

It is actually quite similar with people. For instance, a person might be very good at work. That means they are good at getting difficult things done quickly. They'll also probably be good at telling other people what to do, and maybe they are able to think carefully about money a lot of the time. That person will never miss a meeting and will work a lot—maybe late into the night or over the weekend. But the strengths that make them good at work are also weaknesses. They probably don't have enough time to play or have fun. They are always checking their phone to see if there is a message about work. They might be stressed and worried because they have to make sure that every little work problem gets solved quickly. So this person, even though they're good at doing their job, might not be a lot of fun to be around at home.

You might know a girl or boy who is quite exciting—they make jokes about the teacher, they do not care what their parents think, they are adventurous and quite naughty. But these exciting things about them are also weaknesses: they most likely get into trouble a lot and because they're so busy being naughty, they don't learn much at school. It could even be the other way round—maybe you also know someone who is very careful and neat at school, and is very good at their work, but they're not very brave, and don't like playing games or climbing trees.

There is a big idea here: strengths are also weaknesses. Every strength you or someone else has, is always a weakness, too. You can't be good at one thing without also being bad at something else. Maybe you can see this in yourself. Maybe you get annoyed with yourself for not being so good at some things, but you know you do have talent in other areas. Or suppose, even, that you are good at lots of different things—even that can be a weakness, as it might make you impatient and easily annoyed with other people when they can't do what you can. There's always some way in which the things you are good at make you less good at something else. If you want to see the link yourself, you can play a little game. Write down one list of what you're good at, and write down another list of what you're not so good at—then see how the two lists are related.

The idea that strengths lead to weaknesses tells you something about other people as well. No one is ever going to be perfect. All the things that make someone good will also make them not-so-good in other ways. No one can be the perfect parent or teacher or friend. It's not because they are stupid or useless. It's because they are like that aeroplane: the things that make them great in some ways mean that there are other things they can't be good at. We have to be forgiving of other people's weaknesses, and be forgiving of our own.

# STRENGTHS & WEAKNESSES

*Make a list of your strengths and weaknesses.*
*Once you are done, think about how the two lists are related.*

| WHAT I'M GOOD AT | WHAT I'M NOT GOOD AT |
| --- | --- |
| | |

# An Idea From Ralph Waldo Emerson

Ralph Waldo Emerson was an American philosopher. He was born near the start of the 19th century, in 1803. Emerson did not do very well at school, but later on he went to university and he did much better (this happens to quite a lot of people). Emerson worked as a school teacher for several years, and lived near Boston for most of his life—although he also travelled widely, spending time in France, England and Egypt. He was a great public speaker and gave many lectures to large audiences all over the United States. Emerson was a very kind and gentle man, and was much admired by the president at that time, Abraham Lincoln. Emerson bought a little house in the countryside, near a beautiful small lake, and his friends used to come for long holidays to visit him.

Emerson was interested in how the good things we admire often have drawbacks. For instance, if you are very clever you will probably also be lonely because other people won't understand you. Or, if you have a lot of money you will most likely also have a lot of responsibility. And if you are famous, many people will envy you and you might not have many true friends. Emerson didn't only think this about people. Cheetahs are the fastest land animals—they can accelerate faster than a racing car—but the things that make them so quick, such as being light and thin, make them weak in other ways. A lion, which is much slower than a cheetah, can easily steal a cheetah's food just because it is so much bigger and stronger. Emerson even saw examples of the weakness as strength theory in non-living things. For example, a city that is extremely beautiful, like Venice or Paris, might get so crowded with tourists that it's actually not very nice to visit. By looking at these strengths and weaknesses, Emerson was pointing out something that is quite sad but also very important: nothing can ever be perfect.

# KINTSUGI

You probably haven't heard the word '*kintsugi*' before. That's not very surprising, as most people won't have—though they might have heard about what it means. Kintsugi is a Japanese word, and you say it like this: kin-tsoo-gee. It's made up of two smaller Japanese words: the first part, *kin*, means 'golden', and the second part, *tsugi*, means 'fixing'. When you put the two together, it means repairing a broken thing in a beautiful way. This might sound like quite an odd idea, at first. Normally, if something gets broken, you feel like it has been ruined. You might want to throw whatever it is away and get a new one. But not with kintsugi.

Kintsugi started a long time ago in Japan. The ancient Japanese people loved vases and cups, and they had a tradition of making very beautiful ones, but because they were so fine, they were delicate and they got broken easily. Most owners immediately threw away the broken ones and went out shopping for new ones. But, in the middle of the 16th century, someone had the idea that rather than just throwing away the beautiful pots, cups and bowls, they should try to fix them. People began to fix their broken ceramics, but instead of sticking the bits back together with clear glue, they started to mix the glue with gold dust. This meant you could see very clearly where a pot had been repaired. By doing this, they weren't trying to pretend that the cup or vase had never been broken—they were making it very clear that it had been fixed. They were showing that they didn't mind, and that it was OK to keep hold of something that had once been broken.

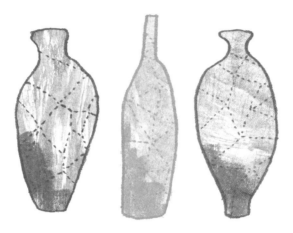

Kintsugi is a big idea. It started from a very small thing—fixing a broken cup—but the same idea can be used for thinking about more important things as well. It is not just cups that can get broken, or bowls or toys or televisions. Actually, the most important things that can get broken are people. When people break it is a funny kind of breaking—it's not just the physical breaking of bones or hurting your body. Breaking can also happen if you get very angry and say something horrible, or if you do something mean. When this happens, you feel as if you have spoiled what was nice and lovely about yourself. Maybe you feel like other people won't want you anymore.

But you can mend yourself in the same way that the kintsugi cups are mended. When you feel sorry about what you did, and say sorry to the person you hurt, it is a kind of mending. You are repairing your feelings. You do not forget that a difficult thing has happened, and you are not pretending that you never said or did that thing—but you're making it better and fixing the problem.

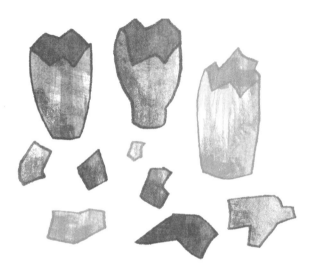

When you make up with someone it can become better than it was before. After you have made up, you can feel sure that an argument will not mean the end of a friendship, and that makes the friendship much stronger. You know, too, that you can be angry with your parents and explain what the problem is and put it right—and that can make your relationship with your parents better than it was before. Knowing that feelings can be mended is very helpful. Sometimes you can't help hurting other people's feelings, and sometimes they cannot help hurting yours. That is never nice. But you don't have to worry about it so much if you keep the idea of kintsugi in your mind.

# WHAT OTHER THINGS COULD BE MENDED AND IMPROVED?

*Make a list of things — other than cups and glasses — that could be fixed.*
*For example:*

○ Using colourful patches to mend your favourite jeans

○ Fixing a friendship by apologising (and really meaning it)

○ Yourself—think of all the times you've fallen over or failed a test. These aren't anything to be embarrassed about! They help you learn and have made you who you are.

○ _____

○ _____

○ _____

○ _____

○ _____

# AN IDEA FROM BUDDHA

Around roughly two-and-a-half thousand years ago, a philosopher called Siddhartha Gautama was born in Nepal (where the Himalayas are). He is better known as Buddha or The Buddha. You have probably heard about him before. Buddha was a prince and his family was very wealthy. When he was growing up he had a very luxurious life—if it was too sunny, he even had servants to hold white umbrellas over him so he could play in the shade. But he wasn't happy. There was so much suffering everywhere in the world. Even insects get trampled on, he noticed.

So when he grew up, Buddha asked himself a very tricky question: how can you stop suffering? One big idea he had was that we should accept that things will never be perfect. People will misunderstand us, we will make mistakes, our friends will sometimes be annoying or mean, our plans won't work out, it will rain when we want to play football, we'll spill hot chocolate over our trousers, we'll get a cold on the first day of the summer holidays. We do not want them to happen, but we are alive on this earth, and these sorts of things are unavoidable. Buddha encourages us to accept these things, rather than getting annoyed by them. If we always want things to be perfect we'll end up being very frustrated and much more sad than we need to be.

Buddha loved the idea of repairing things instead of just throwing them away. He thought that if something was old and worn and broken, you shouldn't see that as a bad thing. Many people were inspired by Buddha's ideas, and some of his followers, particularly in Japan, got very interested in how slightly damaged things can actually be very beautiful—just like a teddy or soft toy can become much more important to you when it's old and loved, and has lost some of its fur.

# THE NEED TO TEACH RATHER THAN NAG

It is not very nice being nagged. Someone will keep on telling you to do something; they keep on asking you, 'Have you done it yet?' and the more they ask the more you don't want to do it. Sometimes you might nag too. You might nag your parents to get a dog or to take you to the cinema to see a film you really want to see. You could ask them every day (or ten times a day) and they never seem to say yes. Although lots of people nag, the funny thing is that it does not work very well. Even if someone says yes eventually, they feel like they have been worn down and forced into something they do not actually want to do. No one really likes nagging, and no one really likes being nagged.

So why do people nag? Basically, the nagger is trying to get someone to do something. They are trying to persuade another person. If you nag, it's because you really want something to happen—you have an idea in your head about how important something is or how nice something could be, and you want the other person to agree. You want them to understand what you understand.

The problem is that nagging isn't a very good way of getting anyone to understand anything. Nagging is like very bad teaching. Imagine you did not understand how to do a new kind of sum in maths. A very bad teacher might keep on saying, 'Why don't you just do it?' They're not explaining. They're not really teaching you at all. They are just nagging.

The big idea here is that when people do not do what others want it is usually because they don't understand properly why it is important. The nagger knows something is important—but they're not explaining why it is a good idea, so no one understands, and no one does it. If you nag or pester or keep on about something, what you are really trying to do (but are not actually doing) is teach someone about what you think and feel.

It can be a bit of a surprise to think that you could be the teacher. Usually you might think of a teacher as someone older who has a special job teaching people. But really, teaching is something that everyone needs to do sometimes. You are a teacher whenever you help someone else understand something—but it might be tricky because adults have not usually spent much time teaching you how to be a teacher.

Think about the best teacher you have ever had. What did they do that was so good? Maybe they were very good at listening to you—they didn't just tell you things, but heard what you had to say. Or maybe they asked you a lot of questions, which means they were trying to find out why you didn't understand something. Probably this good teacher was also very patient—if you didn't understand something, they would not tell you to be quiet or say you were stupid. They were probably enthusiastic, too, and were really excited about sharing ideas with you. Or perhaps the most important thing was that they didn't make you feel bad for not knowing something already. A good teacher remembers that you cannot know a thing until someone teaches you it—so if you don't know something, it's not because you are stupid, it's because no one has been a good enough teacher yet.

So, you probably already know quite a lot about good teaching, because at some point you've had a good teacher. You can learn how to be a better teacher, too, by learning from them. Remember that if you are being nagged, someone is just trying to teach you something—and remember, too, that if you want to explain something to someone, it's better to teach than to nag.

# NAGGING Vs TEACHING

*What other things can you think of that might be changed from nagging to teaching?*
*Look at the examples below and then write some of your own.*

| EXAMPLES OF NAGGING | EXAMPLES OF TEACHING |
|---|---|
| "Go and tidy your room!" | "Tidying your room will make it easier for you to find your things." |
| "Hurry up, you're going to be late!" | "Being on time shows that we appreciate the people or things we're going to see." |
| "You're being a pain." | "Why do you think you're acting like this?" |

# An Idea from Immanuel Kant

In the 18th century there was a philosopher who lived in Germany called Immanuel Kant. He looked quite odd—he was very small and a bit of a hunchback. His family were extremely poor, but he was good at learning and got a job in a university, where he was a very popular teacher. He went to so many parties that his friends worried he wouldn't have time for writing books, but he got up really early in the morning (at five a.m.) and did his writing then. He was very neat and tidy and loved making little rules for his life. He always went for a walk at exactly four o'clock in the afternoon and he had a rule that he had to tell jokes when he was eating a cake or ice cream at the end of dinner. Kant loved gazing up at the stars on clear, dark nights: it reminded him that he was very small and the universe is huge.

Kant hated it when people ordered each other about. He thought that the most important thing was to understand why you have to do something —you should not do something just because someone has told you to, but because you see for yourself that it's a good thing to do. So, if we want to get other people to do things, we have to explain properly what we want. We have to get them to see for themselves why it is such a good idea. Kant thought that if something really was a good idea, then other people would be able to understand why it's worth doing it. If you teach them, you won't have to force them.

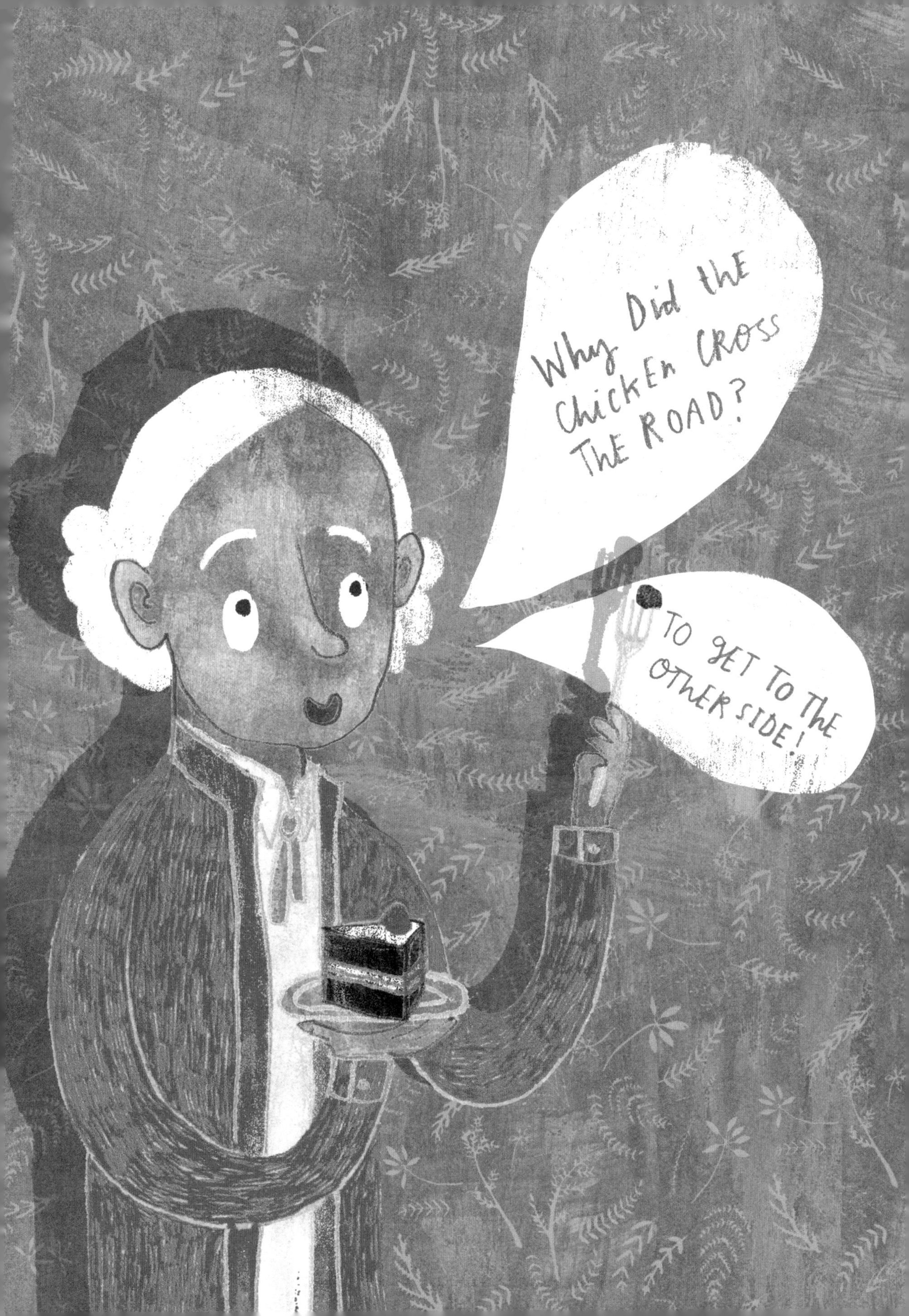
Why Did the Chicken CROSS THE ROAD?
TO GET TO THE OTHER SIDE!

# THE MIND-BODY PROBLEM

How other people think about you depends a lot on how you look. This is quite a strange and sometimes difficult thing to think about—but it's also very important to discuss.

If you happen to look cute and innocent, other people (and especially adults) probably think that you are a very nice and well-behaved person. That might not actually have very much to do with how you feel inside, but they don't know that. If you look messy and crazy, that's probably what other people think you are like, even though you might really be quite careful and thoughtful.

If that doesn't sound very nice, it's worth remembering that you probably think the same things about other people sometimes. If you don't know someone very well, you probably guess what they are like as a person from their appearance. All you have to go on when meeting someone new is what they look like—you do not know anything about what's going on inside their heads.

When it comes to you, though, it's different. You know yourself, and you know that how you look isn't really a very good guide to what you are like. Maybe you don't look exactly the way you would like to. Maybe you think you are too tall or too short, or you wish your nose was different or your hair or your ears; you might worry that you are too chubby or too skinny, or that you don't look enough like other people. Behind all these very different worries is one main thought: other people will get the wrong idea of me—they will not see who I really am, they will just see what I look like.

If you look very carefully at yourself in the mirror and imagine what other people might think about you if they only paid attention to what you look like, it can be quite strange. Imagine someone was trying to guess what you are like. They'd maybe get one or two things right, but they'd

be wrong in lots of ways. There's a very important difference between how you look on the outside and how you really are on the inside.

Try brushing your hair a different way or making a different expression in the mirror. These changes don't actually change you at all—you are still exactly the same person you have always been, but the way your face looks will be sending a different message to people. It's amazing how you can change what people think of you just by altering your look, even though you haven't really changed at all.

But however much you change your hair or pick different clothes or smile or frown, one thing remains pretty certain: other people won't be able to know who you really are just by looking at you. This isn't because other people are stupid—it is because what someone is like inside is always quite hard to get to know.

It is OK to feel a bit sad about this sometimes. You did not choose the way you look, but other people judge you by your appearance. They see your hair or your nose or your legs and decide who you are just on that. That's why it's normal for people to worry about how they look—because they know (sadly) that other people will judge them by it. It is not very fair, but it happens all the time. The funny thing is that this happens to everyone. Everyone has been dumped in a body they did not choose. We didn't choose how we look; yet we keep judging others as if who they are is determined by what they look like.

We can be nicer to others by remembering that inside, people might be very different from the way they look. Someone who looks very smart and boring might also be friendly and funny; someone who is very old and slow might remember exactly what it's like to be a child; someone who speaks in a funny way might have some very important things to say; someone who is really pretty might secretly feel sad and ugly; someone who looks very successful might actually feel like a failure. You can't tell just by looking at them. There's one thing that you do know, though: they're all like you, because they're all different on the inside from the way they happen to look on the outside.

# AN IDEA FROM JEAN-PAUL SARTRE

French philosopher Jean-Paul Sartre was born in 1905, at the beginning of the 20th century. He was unhappy at school, where he got bullied a lot, but went to university and did very well there. He had unusually large ears and his right eye always looked as if it was staring into the corner, and he was also quite naughty and loved playing tricks on people. After university, Sartre became a schoolteacher for a few years and mainly lived in Paris. He liked going to cafés, and loved eating cakes and pastries. He eventually became extremely famous—when he died in 1980, fifty thousand people went to his funeral.

Sartre was very interested in all the odd things about being alive. One of those odd things is that we can experience ourselves in two very different ways: there's the way we are 'for ourselves' and the way we are 'for others'. In our own heads we have memories, plans, ideas and hopes and lots of complicated feelings. But for other people, we might just be someone with glasses who goes to the school down the road. Sartre was worried that we might lose touch with all the interesting things in our own heads and start to think of ourselves just in the way other people see us. We might pay too much attention to what other people think of us.

We don't do it to be horrible, but we often forget that other people are much more interesting than the way they look. You might see your teacher as just a teacher, with a bit of a funny haircut and bad shoes, but inside themselves they're different. They remember being five and playing hide-and-seek, and being twelve and good at gymnastics. They love swimming and going out to dinner with their friends and they dream about climbing mountains in Iceland, learning to ride a motorbike or to dance.

It's very important that we try to think like Sartre, and remember that you can't know what someone is really like just by looking at them—you have to get to know them first.

# WHY YOU FEEL LONELY

Do you ever feel lonely? You probably do, from time to time. Everyone feels lonely sometimes, even if they have friends and family around them—it doesn't mean you're weird.

That's one of the most puzzling things about feeling lonely—it doesn't just happen when there are no other people around. In fact, most of the time we feel lonely when no one else seems to understand us. That's why feeling lonely can make you wonder if there's something wrong with you. Maybe other kids in your class get excited by things that you're not really interested in. Perhaps you really like studying insects or Greek myths and legends (for example), but these things do not seem to interest anyone else. It can make you feel lonely. You can end up feeling that you are a bit odd and that no one understands you.

You are not strange, though, and you are not really all that difficult to understand. It's just that you are surrounded by a very small selection of people: the twenty or thirty children who happen to be in your class, and the handful of people who happen to be in your close family. Such a small group of people does not give you much chance of finding someone who totally gets you. But luckily, there are so many people in the world that there are likely to be lots of extremely nice people who do share your interests and who would love to talk to you about them and join in. Imagine that just one person out of a hundred will be able to really understand you. That doesn't sound like much, but in a city of a million people that means ten thousand—and in a country of sixty million, it means six hundred thousand!

So instead of saying 'No one understands me,' you could say, 'No one who is around right now understands me.' There's a big and very important difference between those two feelings. Even though you are at school

with quite a small number of people, who might not exactly share your interests, you can know that it's not really you who is the problem. The problem is that schools and families are so small—in comparison to how many interesting people there are in the world.

Don't worry though—you don't have to wait forever to meet new friends who like what you like. There's another important thing to remember: although other people do not seem to share your interests now, perhaps they could. Maybe there are other children in your class who would love to talk insects or Greek myths, but they keep quiet about it because they don't think anyone else would be interested. Or, maybe they would like to learn about it, but they haven't had the chance to properly understand how interesting those subjects are yet.

You might feel like you're the only one who feels lonely sometimes, but remember that this isn't actually true. Almost everyone feels a bit lonely, even adults: they just do not mention it, sometimes because they are embarrassed to admit it. There's nothing to be ashamed about though. Everyone is looking for people to understand them, so that they don't feel lonely. We need to remind ourselves that there are people out there that we can feel close to. We might not have found the kind of people we need right now, but they will be out there, and we will find them—especially if we can dare to admit (to ourselves at first) that we are lonely.

# HONESTY ABOUT LONELINESS

*List some of the things you might feel lonely about.*
*Knowing where you feel lonely is the beginning of friendship, because*
*good friends get things about one another that no one else does.*

# AN IDEA FROM MICHEL DE MONTAIGNE

One of the nicest people who ever lived was a French philosopher called Michel de Montaigne. He was born nearly five hundred years ago, in 1533. Montaigne came from quite a rich family—they even owned a little castle—and for a while he had a good job in politics. Mostly, though, he liked spending time in a special room filled with books, in a tower in his castle. He was very fond of the local people, even though they weren't as well educated as him. He felt that growing vegetables or cleaning a house could teach you as much—or more—about life as reading books. He had a little moustache and a beard, and went bald quite young.

Sometimes Montaigne was lonely. He did not like the same things as other well-off people who lived nearby. However, he travelled quite a lot, and by travelling he was able to see how different countries are. Clothes that seem ordinary in one place look very strange somewhere else. The things people eat change a lot depending on where you are. We feel odd, Montaigne realised, because we just don't happen to fit in with what's immediately around us—though we might fit in fine somewhere else.

Then Montaigne did a very interesting thing—he wrote a book about what it was like to be him. He wrote about all the things he liked and that interested him. He was the first person ever to do this. To his great surprise he found that a lot of people really did like it. Not everyone of course—maybe just one person out of a hundred. But in a whole country, that was a lot of people. Maybe his next-door neighbour wasn't interested, maybe the people who lived in the village didn't care, but he'd discovered something very important: lots of people can understand you, you just might not know who they are yet.

# THE MEANING OF LIFE

Asking 'What is the meaning of life?' sounds serious. People sometimes think it's a slightly mad question, or imagine that the answer must be very complicated. Actually it's a very important question and the answer isn't too hard to understand.

The meaning of life is about what makes your life feel interesting and good. It's as simple as that. And to achieve this, what mainly counts is fixing things. When you fix something, you solve a problem that matters to you. You use your intelligence and skill to put something right, to stop it bothering or annoying you. It's nice doing this even in quite small ways. For example, maybe your room is messy and you fix it by tidying it up—it feels lovely when it's done. Or maybe you've had an argument with your mum and you fix it by giving her a hug. What makes life bad is problems, so it makes a lot of sense that fixing problems is the thing we have to do to make life good and give it meaning.

It is not always quite so simple as tidying your room or giving someone a hug though. There are big problems as well as little ones. A big problem is something that's bad for other people as well as for you. To get an idea of what you could do to make your whole life meaningful, you can pick out a big problem that you want to fix (or to help fix, because you don't have to do it all yourself). Weirdly, it does not matter how big or serious the problem feels right now. It could be a question like 'Why can't cities be nicer?' or 'How can people argue less?' or 'Why can't everyone make funny jokes?' or 'Why can't everyone have a nice job?' Or you can just start with something that bothers you—maybe that people leave too much rubbish on the streets, or that your friends spend too much time on their phones instead of talking to you. These things are annoying, but they're more than that—they are problems that need fixing. Your annoyance is getting you to notice something that's not very nice in the world—something that could be fixed. There are lots of problems in the world that need fixing.

You probably won't know how to fix your problem yet (though you might have some interesting ideas), but that does not matter. The earlier you ask yourself about which big problems need fixing (and which you'd like to help fix) the better. It's good to think about this early on in your life, because it gives you an idea of the kinds of skills you could learn that will help you. Sometimes school doesn't feel very meaningful because you think, 'What do I need to learn this for?' Education becomes very exciting when you feel like you need to learn something because it'll help you fix an important problem.

Maybe you will not manage to completely fix a big problem. That doesn't matter either. The point is that you're trying, and that you're helping to fix the problem even if it's just a little bit. Your life feels interesting if you are trying to do something good, and that meaningful feeling depends on what you're trying to do—not just what you manage to complete. You can understand this feeling a bit better by imagining that you are doing a jigsaw. There might be a piece that you can't figure out where to put for a while. It will really frustrate you, but you try and eventually you find the right place. It fits perfectly with the other pieces around it, and it feels great to have finally put it there. You've still not finished the whole puzzle, but you feel like you're making progress.

So, the meaning of life is not something big or scary. It's just the feeling that you are making progress in solving the problems that most interest you—even if you haven't got it all sorted out just yet.

# A LIST OF INTERESTING PROBLEMS

*Make a list of problems that you think are particularly interesting to solve.*
*For example:*

How can we make cities nicer to live in?

Why are some people mean to each other?

What is the best way to live a happy life?

# AN IDEA FROM ARISTOTLE

One philosopher who thought a lot about what makes life feel interesting and satisfying was a man called Aristotle. He lived in Ancient Greece, but was too young to meet Socrates (who we met earlier on page 18). One of Aristotle's jobs was very interesting. He was the teacher of a young prince called Alexander. Alexander soon became king, and he led his army to conquer practically all the most important countries at that time. He was so successful that he became known as Alexander the Great. As you can imagine, it must have been a pretty odd experience for a teacher to see someone they taught go on and conquer the world.

Aristotle was interested in everything. He lived at a time when people did not know much and he set out to find out all sorts of things—like how trees grow, why the wind blows, what's the best kind of government to have, why some people are happier than others, how worms are born, how to persuade people and how thinking works.

One of his big ideas was about skills. We're used to the idea of skill—we know that you can become skilled at shuffling cards (if you practise a lot) or at speaking Arabic (if it is not your usual language). However, Aristotle thought a lot more things were skills. He thought that things like making jokes, keeping calm, being kind and being sensible with money were all skills, too. He was right. People are not born knowing how to do these—they learn. Everyone can learn to be good at these things, it is just that normal school education does not usually concentrate on teaching them.

Aristotle also thought that one of the things we most enjoy is using skill to achieve something that is important to us. We like accomplishing things that feel difficult at first, but which we can deal with if we learn how. When we do this, we feel like our abilities and intelligence are being properly used. Aristotle thought that happiness was about feeling that life is meaningful, and that this was achieved by having an important goal and actively working towards it.

# WHY WE HATE CHEAP THINGS

Do you love pineapples? Do they make you feel absolutely crazy with excitement? Probably not. Lots of people quite like pineapples, but hardly anyone thinks they are amazingly wonderful. Two hundred years ago it was very different. At that time, pineapples were very exciting indeed. If you bought a pineapple you would have a special party and invite all your friends round to admire it—everyone would get to eat a tiny little piece, and they'd talk about it for weeks afterwards.

Why aren't we as excited by pineapples as people were two hundred years ago? They still taste the same—the thing that's changed is their price. Today a pineapple doesn't cost very much, but two hundred years ago they were extremely expensive. In those days, it was very difficult to grow pineapples and keep them fresh on a long sea voyage. They cost as much as a car costs today. They were the most expensive things you could eat.

Eventually, though, people worked out how to grow pineapples quite easily and the price came down. At the same time, people became less and less excited by them. The story of pineapples tells us something about ourselves. When something is rare and expensive we find it exciting. But when something is cheap and easy to get, we stop paying a lot of attention to it. We stop noticing what is actually nice about it.

Think about having a bath. It's quite nice to have a bath, but you probably do not think it's especially interesting. However, for hundreds of years people thought that baths were the most amazing things. They would go on holiday just to have a bath. Baths haven't changed—it's just that it's become easy and inexpensive to have one. We don't think of them as so important—having a bath can sometimes even feel like a bit of a chore. Maybe you hardly think at all about how nice a glass of water can be. It seems pretty boring. But if you've been running around and you get very thirsty and your mouth is dry, when you finally get a sip of water it's amazing. It's only then that you notice how clean and fresh water is and how lovely it feels to drink it. Maybe if water was very expensive and you could only drink it on special occasions as a treat, you'd think water was one of the nicest things you could possibly have.

There is a good trick that you can play on yourself that can help you to remember the value of simple things. Try giving something cheap the kind of attention you'd usually give to something very expensive. You could bite into a potato wedge and really think about how warm and comforting it tastes, as if you were the first person to try it in your entire country. Or you could imagine you are the only person in the world who is allowed to brush their teeth—you'd be amazed by what an interesting experience it is, and how fresh your mouth feels afterwards. Or try imagining that a pencil costs as much as a car—you'll start to notice how clever it is that you can sharpen it and use it to make marks on paper.

We can choose to give attention to anything—no matter how small or seemingly ordinary—and make it in turn much nicer.

# AN IDEA FROM MARY WOLLSTONECRAFT

Mary Wollstonecraft was an English philosopher who was born in 1759, over two hundred years ago. She was raised in London, and her childhood was not very happy because her parents quarrelled a lot. When she was older, she and her sisters opened a school—this was quite a scandal, because at that time a lot of people thought that only boys should get a good education, but Mary Wollstonecraft disagreed very strongly. She was a very good teacher and she wrote a philosophy book for children (one of the chapters in her book is about procrastination—an idea we met earlier on in this book, too). She liked going to parties and became friends with a lot of interesting people. She was very brave—and not too worried about what people might think of her. Once, she travelled to Sweden, Norway and Denmark to try to rescue some treasure that had been stolen from one of her friends.

Mary Wollstonecraft was very interested in how people spend money. She tried to teach people to think hard about what they really wanted before they bought anything. Mary Wollstonecraft called this idea of thinking hard about things being 'rational'. She felt that a lot of well-off people wasted their money on things they did not like or enjoy (she definitely would not have encouraged people to spend a fortune buying expensive pineapples). It is not that she thought it was nice to be poor—she liked wearing nice clothes and was very pleased when she made money from the books she wrote—but she thought that a lot of people forget how nice simple and ordinary things can actually be. She tried to help them remember—and hopefully she can help you remember, too.

# THE NEWS DOESN'T ALWAYS TELL THE WHOLE STORY

You see what's on the news everywhere. It's on television and there are newspapers every day that are filled with articles and photos. Quite often the news is not very nice: there's a war somewhere; an earthquake has happened, or a flood; there's been a bomb; or someone has hurt someone or robbed somewhere. It can be frightening. Sometimes the news is about a famous singer or sportsperson, a rich businessman and the new yacht he's bought, or about politicians making important decisions. There is a lot of news. It can feel like the news is telling you everything that's going on in the world—maybe your idea of what the world is like is made up of things you have seen on the news.

But there is something very strange about the news: it actually misses out nearly everything. Think of all the things that you never see in the newspaper. There wasn't a story about how you had a good time at your friend's house last week, or about the cake your brother made your mum for her birthday, or the funny thing your dad said yesterday or about how lovely it is when someone reads you a story. There are lots of things that happen in your life that are not in the news—and that's just in your life. The same sorts of things are going on for almost everyone. Perhaps two boys in Singapore fell out, then made friends again. That's important— but it wasn't in the news. A girl in South Africa could have thought she'd lost her favourite trousers, but it turned out her mum had put them in the laundry basket. Still not in the news. Probably a cat in Madrid in Spain found a lovely warm windowsill and lay there the whole afternoon, but that didn't even make it into the local papers. There are billions of things like this that happen every day—and none of them are in the news. If they were, you'd get a very different—and more correct—picture of what the world is like.

These kinds of stories do not get talked about in the news because the news usually only includes the stories that are shocking or very unusual. Most of the things that happen in the world aren't really like that. The news tends to concentrate on the bad things that happen in the world, to keep people informed and to keep them interested, but if we watch a lot of news we can begin to feel as if everything in the world is awful. It isn't. Actually, lots of good and wise things are going on as well—it is just that they don't get the same attention as the bad things, so they are harder to notice. Imagine you made a video of the three worst things that happened to you in one day and showed it to your parents—they'd get a totally wrong idea of what the whole day had been like.

When you watch or read the news it is important to remember that it is only usually showing you a very tiny selection of what is going on in the world. The world is not such a bad place—you're just not being shown the good bits.

# AN IDEA FROM JACQUES DERRIDA

Jacques Derrida was a French philosopher. He lived quite recently, from 1930 until 2004. He was born in Algeria on the north coast of Africa, although in those days Algeria was still part of France. He was very keen on football and originally he wanted to make that his career. (Funnily enough, Derrida was very much inspired by another philosopher who we met earlier, Albert Camus. Camus also grew up in Algeria and loved football.) Later on in his life, Derrida moved to Paris to go to university. He wrote a lot of books and became very famous. In his spare time, he loved playing snooker. He was really fond of cats, too, and his hair was usually quite messy.

Derrida was very curious about what people say, and also what they don't say—the things people keep quiet about or don't want to pay attention to. If he was reading a newspaper, he'd always be thinking about all the stories that could be in there but weren't. Why weren't they there?

Derrida thought that people often have big reasons why they ignore things. It's not just a mistake—they're not simply forgetting to mention something. They are doing it so they can keep saying something else— so they can pretend. It's the same sometimes with newspapers and the news: they do not just forget that lots of nice or normal things are going on all the time; they actually want to make it seem like the world is more dramatic and dangerous than it really is.

# ART IS ADVERTISING FOR WHAT WE REALLY NEED

It might seem like a funny idea, but art—the kind of art you see in an art gallery—is rather like advertising. Advertising is very powerful. It's one of the biggest businesses in the world, because lots of huge companies depend on getting people to buy what they are selling. Every day you probably see hundreds of adverts—for pizzas, cars, holidays, chocolate bars, toys, games, watches, handbags, shoes... it can feel like absolutely everything you could possibly need is advertised.

But actually, lots of things do not get advertised—at least, not usually. There are not any normal adverts for being a nice friend, or for getting on well with your mum, or for being kind to your brother or sister, or for recognising what is lovely about trees or clouds or for just being happy on your own. All these things are very important, but they do not usually get advertised. Except they sort of do—in art. You might like making art—drawing pictures, doing collages, painting and making things out of clay—but the art in galleries can seem pretty boring and only for adults. That is not really true, though. Art is for everyone. And art is very good at advertising some of the most important things in life that might get overlooked otherwise.

This painting is an advert for being nice to your brother or sister. It is an advert because by painting it, the artist is saying it is important, and by making it beautiful and appealing, he is trying to get you to want it. The picture doesn't want you to buy a piano or blue dress; it wants you to be kind to a younger child who is being a bit silly, just like the girl is here.

*Piano Practice Interrupted*, Willem Bartel van der Kooi, 1813.

This painting is an advert for looking at clouds. By making the clouds look interesting and pretty, it wants to explain to you how much you might enjoy looking at the sky. It's not trying to get you to buy anything, but it is trying to get you to do something.

*A Landscape with a Ruined Castle and a Church*, Jacob van Ruisdael, 1665–70.

This is an advert for crouching down among weeds and mud, looking closely at blades of grass and seeing how each leaf is a different shape. Looking at this painting should make you think about how interesting it might be to do that, and to pay close attention to the nature around you.

*Great Piece of Turf*, Albrecht Dürer, 1503.

Sometimes a work of art advertises a feeling. This one is an advert for feeling quiet and happy on your own. The artist drew the lines by hand and measured them all perfectly. She enjoyed working alone and concentrating very carefully on her art, so this picture helps remind us of how fun it can be to do something by ourselves.

*Friendship*, Agnes Martin, 1963.

Some people think that advertising is bad because it makes us want things we don't really need. They've got a point—some advertising does do that. But that's not the whole story. There are things we really do need that it's good to be reminded of as well. That's where art comes in—it can make us concentrate on some of the beautiful and important things in life. If you want to make friends with a work of art, a good question to ask is: what nice thing is this advertising?

## AN IDEA FROM GEORG WILHELM FRIEDRICH HEGEL

Georg Wilhelm Friedrich Hegel was a German philosopher who was born just over two hundred years ago, in 1770. He worked very hard at school and almost always got top grades. Later, he became the headmaster of a school and then he was in charge of a newspaper before eventually he became a university professor. He liked to stay up very late and if you had visited him in his flat in Berlin at midnight, you would have found him working hard. He loved playing card games and singing songs with his friends and he wrote enormous, very complicated books. He became very famous indeed.

Hegel liked ideas a lot, but he realised something quite sad about them: we can very easily ignore them. He realised that usually we need to see and feel things before we can get excited. If someone just tells you that the beaches in Australia are great, that probably does not make much difference to you—but if you see a picture it might. The picture shows you the long, wide strip of soft sand, the rocks and waves and the warm sunshine. That makes the idea of a nice beach come alive in your brain. It makes sense if you think about it, because seeing and feeling are very important to us. We see and feel even when we are little babies, but we only start to think when we are older. So what art has to do, Hegel said, is to join up an idea with our feelings. Hegel said that art makes ideas that you can see and feel. And that makes them much more powerful.

# WHY DO SOME PEOPLE GET PAID MORE THAN OTHERS?

People get paid very different amounts of money for the work they do. For some jobs, you get a lot of money, but for others, only a little. Why is there this difference? Why does a top football player or someone in charge of a law firm get paid so much more than a bus driver or someone who works in a café?

Pay does not depend on how nice a job is or how nice the person who does it is. The really important question is: 'How many people can do this job?' If lots of people could do a job quite well then the pay will often be less. Most people could manage to drive a bus or be a waiter or waitress, so if you were running a bus firm or a café and you needed a new worker you wouldn't have to offer much money to get someone to do it.

But suppose you are in charge of a football club and you want your team to win a lot of matches. You have to get the very best players. There will be hardly any players good enough. All the clubs want these people to play for them, so they offer more and more money to attract the very few really talented and skilled players. Or maybe you're the boss at a law firm.

Only a few people know enough about all the different laws to do the job well, and lots of firms would like to hire them. So you would have to offer more and more money to attract the best people. This explains why hardly anyone makes a lot of money. The only jobs that pay really well are jobs that hardly anyone can do well. Any job that a lot of people can do won't be paid very well, because they don't have to convince people to do it—it will just be paid an average, normal amount.

This is also why highly-paid jobs are not always particularly enjoyable. They're usually very stressful. If you're being paid a lot of money, people expect you to be very good at what you are doing, all the time. If a waiter or waitress spills some juice on someone, that's a bit annoying, but it's really quite a small problem. However, if the person in charge of a law firm makes a mistake it could cost the firm millions of pounds. There is always something big that could go wrong—and they know it.

Unfortunately, even if you are very good at something, you still might not make a lot of money. It depends on how much people need you to do it. Suppose you are very, very good at standing on one leg—you can do it for hours. That's amazing. But it's probably not going to make you rich, because there aren't many people who need or want you to do that.

If you want to have a job that pays well, there are two things you have to keep in mind: you have to work out what you can do very well that lots of other people want done, and you have to work out how much you would mind the stress that usually goes with a high-paying job. You also have to remember that lots of jobs which don't pay that well are still very important and fun to do. Some of the greatest artists and writers who ever lived were not very successful when it came to making money. There are lots of important people in the world who are not rich.

# AN IDEA FROM ADAM SMITH

Adam Smith was born in Scotland about two hundred and fifty years ago. He grew up in the countryside and loved exploring the hills and woods. He was pretty good at school and when he was older he got a job teaching in a university. He was a very good teacher. He was interested in kindness and sympathy (being sensitive to what other people are feeling), but he was also very interested in how money works and in how people (and whole countries) can make more money. This was very important to him because when he was younger, Scotland was quite a poor country—not everyone had shoes or enough to eat.

Adam Smith said that the way to make money is to think about what other people need, and then to make those things more cheaply. Everyone needs shoes, for instance, but in Scotland a lot of people didn't have shoes because they cost so much to make (it took a whole day for one person to make a pair of shoes). The trick, said Adam Smith, was to start a shoe factory. Using machines and getting a lot of people organised means that you can make a lot more shoes much more quickly and cheaply, so lots more people can buy them.

Adam Smith realised something rather amazing: if you want to make money, it is not enough just to ask, 'What do people need?' You have to work out how to make a lot of those things cheaply so that they are accessible to the greatest number of people.

# WHAT'S FAIR?

Some families have more and some families have less. Some people have swimming pools, while others do not even have a garden. Some people go on lots of holidays and others have to stay at home. Some houses are huge, but others are not very nice at all.

Is it fair that some people have lots of nice things and others do not? Philosophers have thought a lot about what makes things fair. They are called 'political' philosophers, and they try to work out how the world can be fairer. But before they can do that, they have to ask a tricky question: what is 'fair'? What does 'fair' actually mean?

Imagine you are cutting up a pizza to share with other people. If there are six people it seems only fair to cut it into six pieces that are all the same size. Then everyone will get the same. If you were in charge of the world, could you do the same with money and houses and nice holidays? Would it be fair if you gave everyone exactly the same? You would think so, but maybe not. Some people work much harder than others. Some people have very good ideas that help a lot of other people. Maybe it's OK if they get more. Or what if someone's parents are really quite nice—they help their children lots and listen carefully and take them on interesting trips.

Could you say: 'It is not fair that you have such nice parents because other people do not have such nice parents—your parents should not be allowed to be so good to you'. Or, if someone is really good at maths or running, is that fair? Would you say: 'You'll have to wear very heavy shoes and miss all the maths lessons so that everyone can be the same at running and at maths'? Probably not.

So maybe the idea of making everything the same doesn't really work. Of course there will be some differences. The problem is, how big will they be? To make everything as fair as possible, you'd want everyone to be as equal as possible. Think about this: what if, before you were even born, you were able to look down from the sky at the whole world. You can see all the lives that people are leading, but you don't know which life was going to be yours. You can see all the families, but you don't know which family you might be born into, what house you'll live in or what school you'll go to. You might be lucky and land in a nice place and get some very nice things, or you might be unlucky and get the worst ones.

Looking at one country, you might see some really great places you could land. There are families with helicopters and amazing houses with two swimming pools. But then you notice that most of the families in this country have hardly anything, and most of the schools are crumbling. The chances are that you could end up with something horrible, so that country doesn't seem very appealing.

Then you look at another country. In this country, there are quite a lot of good places (though no one at all owns a helicopter or has two swimming pools). There are hardly any really awful places. Even the people who do not have so much still have enough. Maybe their house is smaller but it's still OK; maybe there is a school that is not quite as good, but it is not that bad. Probably you would think that it's wiser to choose this country —even if you end up getting the worst place here, your life will still be pretty good.

Thinking about countries like this is an interesting test for how fair a country is. Total equality and fairness might not be possible, and not everyone will have the same, but at least in the second country no one is having a really awful time while other people have everything.

# FAIR PLACES TO LIVE

*Imagine yourself before your birth. You can choose any country in the world to live in,*
*but you can't tell whether you will be rich or poor. Where would you choose to live?*
*What does that tell you?*

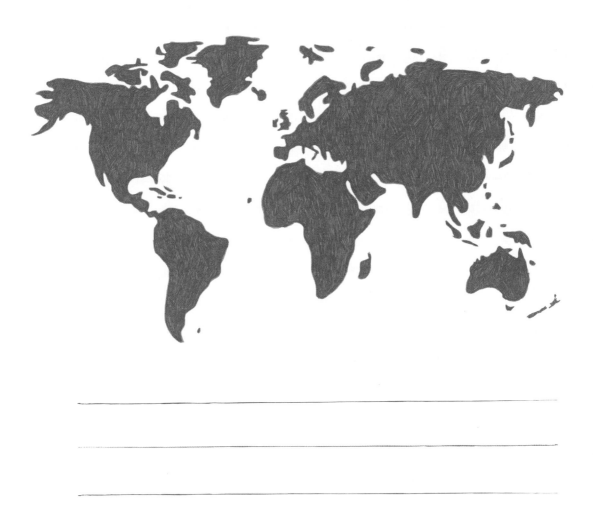

# AN IDEA FROM JOHN RAWLS

There was an American philosopher called John Rawls who lived not too long ago—from 1921 to 2002. That is quite recent for a philosopher, many of whom lived a long time ago. It might seem like all philosophers are ancient, but the good thing about philosophy is that it doesn't really matter when a good idea was thought up. Some good ideas have been around for a long time, while others are quite new—but what matters is how helpful they are to us.

John Rawls grew up in Baltimore in the USA. His family was quite well off and his parents were very good to him, but there were lots of very poor and unhappy people who lived nearby and even as a child he was worried about this. Why was his life so nice when other people had such a difficult time? He decided he'd try to do something about it when he grew up.

One thing that really struck him was that even in countries that are rich, there are usually still a lot of people who have terrible lives. The problem isn't how to make this country richer (it's rich already), but how to split up the good things it already has. Why doesn't that happen? He thought it was because we don't have a shared idea of what's fair. That's why he invented the test that we've just been looking at. He called this the 'veil of ignorance'. Would you think this was an OK country to live in, if you didn't know which bit of it you were going to have to live in? If we have good ideas we can try to solve really difficult problems.

# SHYNESS: HOW TO OVERCOME IT

You probably know quite a lot about shyness. Children very often feel shy around new people. If you start at a new school where you do not know anyone, you probably feel like it's going to be difficult to get to know the other children there—what if they don't like you? Or perhaps one time your mum or dad takes you to visit some of their friends. They seem so different. They come from another country. Maybe they have a daughter who is older than you and has a name you don't know how to say, 'Marie-Christine'. She seems so different. You cannot think of anything to say. You feel shy.

Let's try to look inside shyness and see what it's actually made of. Shyness is the idea that because someone is a stranger, you do not know what to say to them or how to act. With your friends it's usually easy because you already know what they are like—you know what they like talking about and what they like doing. But with a new person, it can feel very hard. That's actually very normal. You just have to find out what they're like. It is not because there's something wrong with you, or with them. You just don't know what they are like, or how they feel comfortable behaving. It is impossible to know that at the beginning—for everyone.

The thing that can make a big difference to how you feel is an idea. Even though another person looks and sounds different and you don't know them, you can be sure that really they aren't different from you. Marie-Christine might do her hair differently to you, and maybe she's never watched any of your favourite TV programmes and is quiet while you are loud, but you probably have some things in common. If you're interested in going camping, you could ask her if she has ever been camping. Or if you like dancing or acting, you could ask if she likes doing those things, too. Probably she won't like exactly the same things (that would be very unusual) but there will be something you are both interested in. And it's good to try to find out. Remember, too, that she probably feels just the same way that you do.

You might not realise it, but a lot of grown-ups get shy too. It's always the same problem. They think that because someone is a bit different, they won't have anything in common. It's not always obvious what you might have in common with someone you've never met before, especially if they come from a different place or are a different age from you, but actually they must have a lot in common with you. Because they are a human being, too. And the same basic things that have happened to you, have happened to them: they've got parents, and friends, they get bored and lonely, they get frightened, they worry about things, they like stories (though you don't know which ones yet), they have hobbies (though you don't know what they are at first), they like going on holiday (but you don't know where). Everyone has these problems and these kinds of interests. So even if you are meeting someone for the first time, you know roughly where to start looking for things you share—even with Marie-Christine.

# AN IDEA FROM MAIMONIDES

Maimonides was a Jewish philosopher who was born in Cordoba, Spain, in the 12th century—more than eight hundred years ago. He was very fond of his younger brother. When he grew up he worked as a doctor in Morocco and then in Egypt, where he became the personal doctor to the sultan, or ruler, of the country. He was interested in how to be a good person and was very impressed by Aristotle, the Greek thinker we met earlier.

Maimonides was very interested in the ways in which people seem so different—they look different, they enjoy different games, they are good at different things, they are different ages, they live in different countries, they like having different things for breakfast, they wear different clothes. We tend to look at other people—or groups of people—and feel 'these people are not like me, I can't understand them or be friends with them'. But Maimonides did not like this attitude. He thought that behind all these differences we are all actually quite similar—we share a lot that's really important. Kindness and love are important to everyone. Everyone wants to be liked and understood (even if they don't say so). The details vary from person to person but the basic picture of being human is the same for everyone. We are actually much more like other people than we usually think. There is no need to be so shy.

# WHY GROWN-up LIFE IS HARD

Have you ever felt sorry for a grown-up? In particular, for your own parents? It sounds a little strange because adults seem to have so many advantages. They can do whatever they want (no school, no bedtimes), they have money, they can drive and they know lots of things. Sometimes, though, you might see them looking worried or sad—or even crying.

What goes wrong with adult life? Quite a lot of things can, once you think about it. Maybe an adult ends up doing a job they don't like that much. They have to spend a huge part of their life at work, doing the job they don't enjoy. It's not easy to stop doing it, because they need the money and it is tricky finding something better. They feel that they could be doing something better with their life. They might have talents they have not properly developed. Or perhaps they feel like they married the wrong person. It seems as if that would be a hard mistake to make, but it's not really. It's like making friends with someone but it turns out you don't have much in common. You may have experienced that before. But when you get married, it's a much bigger problem because you might have children with them, or share a house together, and you would feel terrible about leaving all of that. Adults often worry about money, too. Maybe they spend too much, or maybe they don't make enough. Another of the big things that bothers adults is getting older. At the moment, you probably feel like you have endless time stretching out before you, with so many possibilities for what might happen. Adults often feel like they don't have enough time—they've already lived half of their life or more. They feel that time is running out.

It is possible to manage the problems of adult life better. But it's tricky. People don't teach you how to do it. You need a lot of skills: how to choose who to get married to, how to deal with money, how to choose a job you really like, how to face the fact that you are getting older every day and are going bald. Generally people don't get taught these skills. It's a bit like being asked to fly a plane without having any lessons first. It's not impossible to fly a plane, but you can't do it without any preparation—you need to learn the skills. You need a lot of skills to be an adult, but adults aren't usually taught them.

Quite often grown-ups see children as 'innocent'. They don't really mean that children are lovely and sweet all the time (they're not that stupid). What they mean is that children don't yet know about some of the normal, difficult things that come with growing up. Adults don't often tell children about their problems. That's understandable: they're trying to be kind and stop you from worrying about the future, so that you can enjoy what's going on now.

But maybe there's another idea. Maybe, if you learn about the normal troubles of adult life now, before they happen, you will see that they are not so scary after all, and you can learn how to deal with them better when the time comes.

# AN IDEA FROM... PHILOSOPHY

Philosophy is one of the ways that we deal with the difficulties of life. One of the main ways that it helps us is by giving us information about things before we desperately need it, so that we can be prepared. Rather than only concentrating on what is happening right now, we have to be brave and look quite carefully at the things that will happen in life later on —and to see what might go wrong. We don't have to deal with those things straight away, but one day we will. So there's no point in pretending they will not happen.

We're not doing this to make ourselves miserable now, though. It's not trying to ruin the happiness we have at the moment by realising that we might have a bad time later. Actually, it is the opposite. If you have an idea of the challenges you'll face early on, you can start to develop the skills you will need to cope with them. It's a bit like climbing a very high mountain. If you think it's going to be easy and fun, you will be shocked to find out that actually, it's pretty difficult. But if you train beforehand by walking up lots of smaller mountains, and you talk to people who've done it already (and who have made plenty of mistakes along the way), you can learn from what's happened to them and prepare yourself. You need a kind of mountain-climbing friend who can give you information in advance and teach you the skills you need.

Philosophy is rather like this—but obviously it's not got anything to do with climbing mountains. Philosophy is about how we face the normal difficulties of adult life. It's not frightened about how tricky life can be —it's got loads of experience, and has done it all before.

In this way, philosophy is a kind of 'life-friend'. It is not a person—it's a whole group of people and their ideas. They've faced a lot of troubles and tried to learn how to deal with them. This book tries to give you some ideas about how you can understand life, and how to make it a bit easier than it sometimes turns out to be. That's what philosophy tries to do, too.

# LIST OF THINKERS

### Buddha

563 BC – 483 BC

Taulihawa, Nepal

### Confucius

551 BC – 479 BC

Lu, Zhou (now China)

### Socrates

470 BC – 399 BC

Athens, Greece

### Aristotle

384 BC – 322 BC

Athens, Greece

## Seneca

4 BC – AD 65

Rome, Italy

P 44

## Hypatia of Alexandria

360 (approx) – 415

Alexandria, Egypt

P 68

## Ibn Sina (Avicenna)

980 – 1037

Bukhara, Persia & Hamadan, Iran

P 34

## Maimonides

1135 – 1204

Morocco & Egypt

P 144

## Michel de Montaigne

1533 – 1592

Guyenne, France

P 110

## René Descartes

1596 – 1650

France, Netherlands & Sweden

P 60

### Zera Yacob

1599 – 1692

Emfraz, Ethiopia

P 40

### Matsuo Basho

1664 – 1694

Osaka, Japan

P 50

### Jean-Jacques Rousseau

1712 – 1778

Switzerland & France

P 74

### Adam Smith

1723 – 1790

Edinburgh, Scotland

P 134

### Immanuel Kant

1724 – 1804

Königsberg, Prussia (now Russia)

P 98

### Mary Wollstonecraft

1759 – 1797

London, England

P 120

## Georg Wilhelm Friedrich Hegel

1770 – 1831

Berlin, Germany

P 130

## Ralph Waldo Emerson

1803 – 1882

Massachusetts, U.S.A

P 86

## Friedrich Nietzsche

1844 – 1900

Switzerland & Germany

P 80

## Ludwig Wittgenstein

1889 – 1951

Vienna, Austria & Cambridge, England

P 24

## Jean-Paul Sartre

1905 – 1980

Paris, France

P 104

## Simone de Beauvoir

1908 – 1986

Paris, France

P 30

## Albert Camus

1913 – 1960

Algeria & France

P 54

## John Rawls

1921 – 2002

Massachusetts, U.S.A

P 140

## Jacques Derrida

1930 – 2004

Algeria & France

P 124

## THE SCHOOL OF LIFE

The School of Life is a global organisation helping people lead more fulfilled lives. It is a resource for helping us understand ourselves, for improving our relationships, our careers and our social lives — as well as for helping us find calm and get more out of our leisure hours. We do this through films, workshops, books and gifts — and provide a warm and supportive community. You can find us online, in stores and in welcoming spaces around the globe.

www.theschooloflife.com

## LIST OF ARTWORKS P128 – P129

## IMAGE CREDITS P151–P155